WHAT PEOPLE ARE SAYING ABOUT

MEETING EVIL WITH MERCY

This book is a real treasure... What a beautiful and sensitive way the author interprets the work of the late Anglican priest, Martin Israel. In this careful study of his life, Philip Pegler offers a compelling and meditative template for our time – and these searingly beautiful and honest meditations anchor the soul to what is real and true... I feel sad that I never met Martin Israel, but I feel deepened by my experience of such a skilful rendition of his words.

Stephanie Sorrel, author of *Depression as a spiritual journey*

Your book is full of provoki   ave a strong sense that your rew   have done to Martin Israel and ir   you have faithfully represented   y and teaching. Certainly I have an impression   as an original and humble (different from falsely modest) searcher after truth, who bore witness with integrity.

Charles Becker, psychotherapist and counsellor

For anyone interested in a Christian response to the problem of evil, Philip Pegler's book gives us a searching look at the life of Martin Israel, who was born in a prosperous Jewish family, left his native South Africa to become a doctor in London, converted to Christianity and was ordained as an Anglican priest in his forties. His personal passage through darkness and despair and his extraordinarily early mystic experiences made him an authoritative counsellor for the 'perplexed, the harassed and the fearful'. His ministry spoke directly to the heart of Philip, who had suffered his own 'dark night of the soul' – and the radical teaching that the only enduring answer to atrocity is to 'bid evil welcome' is balm for those, who, like the author, wonder whether the fierce heat of authentic experience can indeed bear good fruit.

Philip Pegler recounts the evolution of this spiritual journey against the background of Martin Israel's unusual and sometimes alarming life story, which included abuse during his childhood, an episode of acute illness and a near-death experience as well as paralysing shyness and isolation as a young man, and points to the central place given in Israel's counselling to the fostering of the inner life. He emphasised the need to accept our own darkness and live creatively with the baleful influences in the world so as to immerse ourselves in the 'sea of gratitude for the privilege of being alive in the present moment'.

The idea that 'evil is an integral part of creation' may or may not be shared by the reader, but the corresponding idea that 'darkness is the most fertile medium of growth' is surely a comforting one, since we all experience times of hopelessness.

Etain Addey, deep ecologist and author of *A Silent Joy – The Diaries of an Italian Hill Farm*

Through dedicated contemplation of the wise teachings of Martin Israel and the application of that wisdom in his own life, Philip Pegler has written a book that offers all of us an answer to the horror of atrocity we are faced with within our world and ultimately within ourselves.

Philip's insightful and tender account of a man who not only taught a rare courage but also lived it with resolute faith and trust – along with the author's skilful guidance and demonstration of how we may apply these timeless teachings – calls to those who find themselves despairing at the darkness in our midst. Like a beacon in the night, this book lights the way ahead for us and I would highly recommend it...

Mike Jenkins, author of *The Escape Artist's Handbook* and founder of the blog *Nothing Saying This*

I absolutely love what you have written. It is very special indeed and I know Martin woud have loved it. You write so well and so clearly – and you frame Martin's character perfectly. Furthermore your book gives articulate expression to the fundamental conviction by which he lived – that despite every appearance to the contrary in our troubled world, ultimately all shall be well...

What I loved about Martin was his simplicity, he was at peace with the totality. There was nothing to add or take away – he was bonded with each moment as it appeared. He sought nothing and lived free of the burdens and distractions of our modern-day living. It was a gift he shared and always with a smile. You too knew that special smile of his and I am glad you are now making his teachings freshly available to the wider world.

Marina, Viscountess Cowdray, close family friend of the late Rev. Dr. Martin Israel

Meeting Evil with Mercy

An Anglican priest's bold answer
to atrocity

Reflections upon the ministry of Martin Israel

Meeting Evil with Mercy

An Anglican priest's bold answer
to atrocity

Reflections upon the ministry of Martin Israel

Philip Pegler

CHRISTIAN
ALTERNATIVE

Winchester, UK
Washington, USA

First published by Christian Alternative Books, 2016
Christian Alternative Books is an imprint of John Hunt Publishing Ltd.,
Laurel House, Station Approach,
Alresford, Hants, SO24 9JH, UK
office1@jhpbooks.net
www.johnhuntpublishing.com
www.christian-alternative.com

For distributor details and how to order please visit the 'Ordering' section on our website.

Text copyright: Philip Pegler 2015

ISBN: 978 1 78535 306 2
Library of Congress Control Number: 2015956004

A CIP catalogue record for this book is available from the British Library.

Design: Stuart Davies

Printed and bound by CPI Group (UK) Ltd, Croydon, CR0 4YY, UK

We operate a distinctive and ethical publishing philosophy in all areas of our business, from our global network of authors to production and worldwide distribution.

CONTENTS

The joy of baptism – Martin Israel with baby, Peregrine Pearson.
West Sussex, England, 1995

Keep thy mind in hell and despair not... If the kings and rulers of the nations knew the love of God they would never make war.

War comes to us for our sins, not because of our love. The Lord created us in His love and bade us live in love and glorify Him.

If those in high places kept the commandments of the Lord and we obeyed them in humility there would be a great peace and gladness on earth, whereas now the whole universe travails because of the ambition for power and the lawlessness of the proud.

Staretz Silouan

1866-1938

from: *The Undistorted Image*

Preface

I dedicate this book with respect and affection, not only to Martin Israel but also to Clare Cameron, who introduced me to his work. Both these gifted and unconventional mystics were first and foremost remarkable human beings – representing the very best of humanity. My two similar studies of their illumined lives and teachings may be regarded as companion volumes, and testify to the essential worth of these two outstanding spiritual teachers – as I pay tribute to their great love, goodness and sense of beauty. In the dark and deeply troubled era which we are presently traversing, they provide a clear and safe path for us to follow. If with their shared gift of foresight, either Martin or Clare were aware of how valuable for my own quest their sane and balanced examples of engaged spirituality would prove, then they gave little hint of it. Silence sometimes speaks far more eloquently than words – I now know this from my own challenging experiences, for which I will ever remain grateful. Nevertheless words still have great power and rich gems of written spiritual instruction may also sustain us in trust and enfold us in mercy.

Keep thy mind in hell and despair not...

This inspiring idea, which is to be found in the invocation at the start of this book, occurred suddenly one day on Mount Athos in Greece to Staretz Silouan, a twentieth-century Russian saint in the Christian Eastern Orthodox monastic tradition. It was a penetrating insight – a blessed outcome of his solitary interior struggle with temptation – that has afforded solace to many a pilgrim on the spiritual path. And it is a potent sentence that memorably encapsulates too the substance of this work, while evoking with sober poignancy the essential spirit of the teachings of both Clare Cameron and Martin Israel.

Philip Pegler,
Midhurst, West Sussex – September 2015
www.hiddenbeautyoflife.com

Acknowledgements

I have drawn with considerable benefit from no less than fifteen books written by Martin Israel to prepare this synthesis of his life and teachings – and my account would have been both colourless and insubstantial without the quotations carefully chosen from them, which begin almost every chapter and in addition furnish the text with invaluable detail.

Each one of these title is given below in order of publication with due gratitude and acknowledgement to its respective publisher for the often brief but sometimes numerous extracts selected from its particular pages. Similarly I gratefully acknowledge the publishers of other books listed here, from which I have quoted.

Martin Israel, *Summons to Life*, (London: Hodder and Stoughton, 1974).

Martin Israel, *Precarious Living*, (London: Hodder and Stoughton, 1976).

Martin Israel, *Smouldering Fire*, (London: Hodder and Stoughton, 1978).

Martin Israel, *The Pain That Heals*, (London: Hodder and Stoughton, 1981).

Martin Israel, *Living Alone*, (London: SPCK, 1982).

Martin Israel, *The Spirit of Counsel*, (London: Hodder and Stoughton, 1983).

Martin Israel, *Healing as Sacrament*, (London: Darton, Longman & Todd, 1984).

Martin Israel, *Coming in Glory*, (London: Darton, Longman & Todd, 1984).

Martin Israel, *The Dark Face of Reality*, (London: Collins, Fount Paperbacks, 1989).

Martin Israel, *The Quest for Wholeness*, (London: Darton,

Longman & Todd,1989).

Martin Israel, *Life Eternal*, (London: SPCK, 1993).

Martin Israel, *Dark Victory*, (London: Mowbray, Cassell imprint, 1995).

Martin Israel, *Angels*, (London: SPCK, 1995).

Martin Israel, *Doubt*, (London: Mowbray, Cassell imprint, 1997).

Martin Israel, *Happiness That Lasts*, (London: Cassell, 1999).

John Wyborn, *Martin Israel – An Appreciation*, (Louth, Lincolnshire: CFPSS, 2013).

Archimandrite Sofrony, *The Undistorted Image*, (London: The Faith Press, 1958).

Scriptural Quotations: The New English Bible, (London: Oxford and Cambridge University Presses).

* * *

On a personal level, my grateful thanks are due to my loyal, loving wife, Wendy and to my patiently obliging brother, Christopher as well as to steadfast, old friends – Charles Becker, Etain Addey, Stephanie Sorrell, Mike Jenkins, Jennifer Malone and Iain Colquhoun, whose creative wizardry regarding graphic design never ceases to impress me. Iain's delicate photograph of a fallen birch leaf on a background of brambles adorns the front cover of this book, reminding me that dead leaves and sharp brambles alike find their rightful place within the abundance of Nature.

I will always marvel too how the manuscript came to the attention of such an eminent churchman as the Rt Rev. Michael Marshall, assistant Bishop of London, who knew Martin Israel personally and kindly agreed to provide the Foreword. This could never have happened without an unexpected encounter in the woods near our home with his spiritual walking companion, the Rev. Soon-han Choi, who kindly and most attentively acted as go-between. It is amazing what miracles can occur when you are out simply walking the dog.

I greatly appreciate too the steady encouragement of Marina, Viscountess of Cowdray, whose family supported Martin during his latter years of failing health, and who most generously gave me permission to use as frontispiece an evocative photograph from the family album, showing Martin, together with her eldest son, the Honourable Peregrine Pearson as a baby during his christening at St. Mary's Church, Easebourne in May, 1995.

I acknowledge wholeheartedly the sound advice of Tim Ward, my editor at Changemakers Books, who believed in my first book – *Hidden Beauty of the Commonplace* – and helped me craft this second one, before stepping aside to allow Christian Alternative to take over publication. I finally proffer thanks to all members of the dedicated, creative team I have been allocated by John Hunt, who have been responsible for its smooth production.

Foreword

The transformation from *'self-interest to self-sacrifice on behalf of the world'* could well be the strap-line for a biography of Martin Israel – priest and doctor – as well as constituting a radical summons to the contemplative life, rooted and grounded in prayer, of which Martin was both a disciple and an apostle. But, Philip Pegler's book – *'Meeting Evil with Mercy'* – is so very much more than simply a biography about a 'highly gifted yet totally unpretentious' medical doctor and priest.

Converting from a Jewish family to Christianity, and subsequently following his medical training and practice as a doctor, Martin quarried deeply into the seams of mystical theology and was subsequently ordained as an Anglican priest. Not surprisingly, Martin suffered the fate of many who bridge two apparently contesting disciplines, yet in so doing, was singularly obedient to that double mandate of Christ 'to preach the gospel and heal the sick.'

For me, it is both the incredible relevance and urgent summons which mark out this well-crafted book for a wide readership in today's dark and deeply troubled world, where the perilous forces of evil are only all too evident, no less today than during Martin Israel's lifetime, and frequently and ironically in the name of 'religion!'

'When the foundations are being shaken, what can the righteous do?' asks the psalmist of old. Whether it be the 'foundations' of his personal life, through major physical and mental breakdowns which Martin suffered together with the 'black dog' of deep depression, fuelled by destructive childhood experiences, or the horrors of the holocaust and ethnic cleansing hideously rampant in Martin's lifetime in the world at large, in all this, Martin consistently re-affirmed that (in the words of St. Paul) we wrestle not simply 'against flesh and blood' but against 'principalities and the powers of darkness,' and in so doing are necessarily compelled to participate in nothing less than the triumph of Christ's victory – a victory won, however, not with the weapons of this world, but with the power of mercy and love in the face of evil and darkness. To do this requires a disciplined life sacrificially consecrated to contemplative prayer and expressed in costly service and ministry to others (anything but escapist!) – a 'spiritual path of loving kindness and non-violence' – indeed, a 'road less travelled' and most certainly anything but easy to emulate.

I was privileged to know and to meet Martin on several occasions, and to benefit from his ministry – a ministry of deliverance and a ministry of discernment. On both occasions, Martin spoke and ministered effectively with that quiet, unselfconscious yet self-authenticating authority which is the fruit of a life in the Spirit, spanning not only the world of sense and sight, but that greater world beyond, to which Martin was no stranger.

In this and so many other ways – not least his leading of retreats, in which he spoke without notes and clearly *in* the Spirit, rather than just *about* the Spirit – Martin was a prophet before his time. The last few decades of the last century, were years when, in many parts of the church, we lost our nerve in the credentials and the gifts of the Spirit with which Christ has empowered his church, and all in favour of 'programmes', practical 'hands-on' outreach (all of which have their place), but which must not, as Martin frequently emphasised, ever be to the neglect of the inner life of the Spirit in which the deep purposes of God are revealed.

Philip Pegler's outstanding book, will serve as a 'teaser' to re-introduce a wider public (not least the clergy) to Martin Israel's many written works; to renew and refresh the churches of God, in order to recover the vision of that mandate, once-for-all given to the disciples, to 'preach the gospel and to heal the sick', to bring, both *in* the Spirit and *by* the Spirit, uncreated light to places of darkness; a deep healing for the nations of the earth, divided and torn by prejudice and hatred, and all this by 'Meeting Evil with Mercy' and the 'love of God spread abroad in our hearts by the Holy Spirit.'

As something of a latter day disciple of Martin Israel, I cannot commend this book too highly for its challenge and relevance for the church, as well as for the world at large, praying, when I studied the manuscript, that even in our day, we might yet experience a fresh Pentecost and a spring time of loving to which the life of Martin so effectively witnessed.

Michael Marshall – Hon. Assistant Bishop in the Diocese of London

Introduction

Saving the World

There is nothing imprecise about the hidden principles that govern the universe, just as there are no mistakes in the working out of natural law here on earth. Despite all agonizing appearances to the contrary in a world of great beauty but immense sorrow, the unrelenting fact remains that we live in an absolutely just realm where cause and effect reign supreme. So much is wrong – injustice and grievous afflictions are plainly seen to be simply everywhere – and yet everything is just as it needs to be. How is this possible?

Faith is hardly amenable to reason, but even so what you notice around you depends on how you look. When you view things deeply with the eyes of love and in the light of faith, you will find signs of great goodness breaking through on all sides – clear evidence of a merciful background, which is the invisible foundation of all activity, whether wholesome or pernicious.

Silent and ignored, because it can only be intuitively known and defies scientific scrutiny, still this *ground of being* endures in the midst of both cynical disbelief and unquenchable hope. This deepest truth insists even in the midst of the heedless destruction of war – in pain too terrible to contemplate – but it can only be contemplated then in the obscure darkness of a faith unadorned by the niceties of creed or ritual and lit up simply by love.

Difficult as it is to accept as a basis for a realistic world view, nevertheless the background peace in the unseen ever remains untouched by vicious hatred, cruelty or oppression. In the manifest world on the other hand, things are ever changing – constantly in flux – governed it seems by an increasingly dangerous volatility. Here, in the challenging foreground of daily life where we all need to function, one crisis follows another. There is precious little time left to attend to the root of suffering, which is ignorance of the way things truly are in reality.

Nobody – whosoever they may be and whatever their station in life – is spared the fleeting pleasures and intermittent discomfort of physical embodiment. Modern living imposes a level of stress inconceivable to previous generations and our intransigent human nature does much to enhance our woes.

Yet in just the same manner as night follows day, so alert intelligence flows naturally from healthy living. We should never forget how much has been achieved with skill and unselfish dedication in the field of human endeavour. Nevertheless we can hardly deny the fact that some aspects of normal, contemporary living – currently regarded as acceptable and harmless enough – are in fact totally unsustainable and even perverse because they are contrary to our best interests. Perhaps it is simply a denial of the straight facts of our human predicament through lack of clear sight that is costing us most dear.

It is striking too how the simplest of questions are often the most difficult to answer. What is the wisest way to greet such apparently widespread indifference to things that really matter? How best may love be sustained in the face of hostility and hatred forgiven while maintaining utter integrity regarding condemnation of violence and the absolute requirement to stand fast in the face of oppression?

The answers are challenging in the extreme and do little to console us. Often it is suffering alone that will open our eyes to the deepest issues of life and death – while sometimes only absolute outrage at the atrocities we witness around us by way of the veritable bombardment of information from the mass media that invades our lives will pierce a sense of apathy and open our hearts to God's mercy.

Ever wary of attachment to extreme opinions, we can at least always begin by taking a firm stand on the most noble of ideals. In such a restive and rapidly shifting era as our own, is it not the bounden duty of all of us who share these concerns somehow to find time in our busy lives to wrest out the space and opportunity to pay tribute to the highest good of which we can conceive – God, Reality or Truth – no matter how we may term it?

That much we *can* do, for whether we like it or not, the quality of life we need to foster as part of a global community depends on the nobility of our aspiration and willingness to cooperate with harmonious intent in furtherance of the cherished aim of establishing a society ruled by sane principles of justice and freedom. And to celebrate whatever is true and of good report, wherever it may be unearthed, is the best way to ease our pain and remove the heavy stone that blocks the source of creativity within us.

It is a tall order, but such a decisive action as making a solemn pledge to honour *everything* in our experience is enough to allow the waters of Life to flow unencumbered – and then all can be renewed in beauty despite inevitable hardship as we face up to our responsibilities with fresh courage.

We cannot predict what will happen when we finally stop resisting the forward thrust of living, because our surroundings and everyone we meet are affected differently by what we do and have their own freedom of choice to respond to our behavior. Certainly we do not live in isolation but truly belong to one another. Life is indivisible because everything is interrelated, and plainly there can only be one totality. The desperate tragedy of modernity is the essential fact that human beings are an inescapable part of reality – and yet do not realise their innate solidarity and suffer accordingly from the unremitting and unacknowledged anguish that only the lack of plenitude and sense of separation from wholeness of being can bring.

The most important thing to remember is that we never need be afraid. Life is pure in essence and benign in purpose. How could the mysterious and mighty power, which created the universe, be other than supremely beneficent? Once we appreciate this, we are set free to decisively play a small but not insignificant part in a more wondrous plan than anyone can envisage. It is an unobtrusive way of service to the wider community in a world, entrancing in beauty but overwhelmed by strife and sorrow.

Then all will be well with us, but we need not imagine that our personal life will somehow end there or cease to unfold. Not at all – it will continue to be just the way it is, but now we shall view it differently as the great mystery of the unknown. It is a profound mystery about which we may never cease to wonder, even as we gain confidence to explore it in awe and delight – more wide awake than before, but less heedless and more responsive to the stark challenges we face.

There is always work to be done – the noble work of unassuming goodness – and it is within the scope of almost everyone to contribute in this way as best they can. Furthermore it is always *this moment* – the task immediately at hand – that claims our attention. For every single person in each living moment, there is no other place but here – and no time like the present. We are already living in eternity. It is certainly an uncomfortable paradox, but the best way to save the world is to see that at the most profound level, the world does not really need to be saved.

Chapter 1

Venture of Faith

We live in a world of darkness which is illuminated by our own courageous movements towards a light, which though within us, is concealed from the eye of reason. Yet in giving of ourselves in hope beyond reason – and this is a venture of faith – we glimpse a depth of reality in ourselves which is the true self, also called the soul. What we would aspire to if we only had the wisdom to do so, would be to live under the direction of the soul, for its dominion is free and joyous.

Anchored deep within us is an undeniable knowledge of our own existence and this immediate awareness is a direct intimation of our own immortal being in the midst of physical impermanence – even as it points to a profound truth inherent in every living moment that is always seeking to find expression.

All of Nature – all created things in fact – speak eloquently like this of eternity ever present in the midst of change to reveal innumerable, sparkling facets of the one ultimate reality.

In this absolute reality is to be found ineffable goodness, as well as tender mercy and above all great love – all essential qualities by which God is known. These divine qualities may be obscured by conflict and suffering, but they are never entirely lost.

As the conviction deepens within us that the supreme creative power, which brought us into being means no harm – and can actually be trusted – our attitude to the challenges we meet on the often stony path of life changes accordingly. And as it does so, we cannot help but proceed further in the fervent wish to give tangible form to this poignant vision of wholeness that will never leave us bereft once we have glimpsed it.

It is a venture of faith as the text introducing this first chapter suggests, but it will also prove to be a stern test of our fidelity regarding that most precious insight we have glimpsed in our heart of hearts. We are not separate from the Absolute – and never have been. This is what mystical unity with God signifies.

* * *

The quotation at the beginning comes from the prolific writings of a highly gifted but unpretentious figure, who is the subject of this biographical study. A remarkable Christian priest by the name of Martin Israel, who originally trained in South Africa and practised as a medical doctor in London, he indicated in incisive fashion forty years ago how we live in a *world of darkness*.

Of course that world was already by then an unpredictable and dangerous place in all sorts of respects and on every level – how could it have been otherwise? But now in addition it has become marked out by the violent upsurge of religious fundamentalism, as well as by overt nationalism; to our great consternation indeed our own era is turning out to be one of distinct menace as the blind, irrational forces of the universal unconscious mind – so long denied and ignored in fear – are surging up to overwhelm the ordered rationality by which any civilized person still aims to manage affairs with justice, compassion and basic respect for human rights.

Little has really changed nowadays except that the stark issues confronting mankind have become more pressing. Even so it has clearly become essential to investigate yet again – as Martin did in a uniquely articulate way – how we may not only summon all the resources at our disposal, but also invoke the spirit of compassion anew. And to attempt this urgent task while still bound to a tired vocabulary that has all but lost the power to truly inspire. What more can possibly be done now to make a difference?

In the weary eyes of the world, to meet evil with mercy seems surely a futile act of utter foolishness. In actual fact it is nothing of the kind. It is really a gesture of the highest wisdom, but it *does* take the greatest courage of all – for when once you determine to take a firm stand on the bedrock of reality, all that does *not* belong to Truth rises up in fury to dissuade you from the most noble of intentions.

To meet evil with fortitude nevertheless is to *dare to greet evil* and go further still. It is actually to *bid evil welcome* and in so doing to disarm its threat at the most fundamental level. And this of course is to follow faithfully the supreme teaching of Jesus Christ – to offer the other cheek to your adversary and to travel the extra mile to help your neighbour in the midst of trouble.

Naturally, the authentic spiritual path of loving kindness and non-violence that you will find outlined in this book is anything but easy to emulate. It has many adherents, but little credibility in terms of effective action from a wordly standpoint. Yet ultimately it is the only enduring *answer to atrocity* – and it was the bold reply Martin Israel unstintingly provided to all who cared to listen during the course of his remarkable healing ministry.

* * *

Undue piety holds little appeal for the modern mind, and extreme religious fundamentalism is the scourge of our time and is wisely shunned by all normal people. Simple goodness and great bravery on the other hand speak directly to the heart and will never go out of fashion. Such fine qualities are rightly celebrated whenever they are seen to gleam in the shadows, and no effort to translate high ideals into practice amidst the abrasive demands of daily life is ever wasted.

Anything we may ever need to know – all the sustenance we will ever need – resides within these hidden depths of our own being, and yet almost certainly we will still need to avail ourselves of sound outer guidance in order to realise that this is so. Such is an unavoidable paradox of the quest for Truth and why it is always valuable to pay tribute to men and women of outstanding wisdom and courage, who are the genuine teachers of humanity. It is they who embody the age-old perennial philosophy expressing the essential truth underlying all the great world religions. By their unselfish example, these noble exemplars of deep wisdom remind us of our innate nobility – and never has this been more urgent than in our own era of rapid change and unremitting turbulence.

I have done so once before, and now once again find myself prompted to relate aspects of my own life story within the warm glow shed by the radiance of another spiritual teacher. But before I embark upon yet another creative journey, it becomes clear to me that I need to question my motivation and intentions. When deep contemplation precedes our most important decisions, the quality of our work is enriched immeasurably.

When we feel moved in admiration to write about someone else, in the beginning our work is clearly derivative. Yet if what we express is a genuine response to the beauty that has touched us and partakes of honesty and candour, it becomes authentic in its own right. When one decisively speaks out in truth it is as if the whole world rejoices.

If a writer feels the need to shelter behind someone else's philosophy, it is probably because they are still in the process of formulating their own convictions – and there is no harm in that. For to borrow from the authority of someone more experienced than oneself is to be involved in a rich learning process and the eventual contribution to a particular field of study becomes all the more valuable. For my part – as long as I live – I trust that I will not become complacent or cease to learn.

Finally we may see how the careful study of another human being acts as a mirror, reflecting our own responses and prompting us to question more deeply how we ourselves function. Informed and uplifted by the example of others, we are enabled to become more deeply rooted in our own reality. We are encouraged to move from a merely personal to a universal vision – and our concern can then embrace the entire world.

Chapter 2

In Quest of True Purpose

Man struggles to keep alive yet often forgets to live. He is obsessed with acquiring things, yet he seldom has the time or understanding to enjoy them. The will to survive is a prerequisite for life, but if the object of the living is simply to escape or postpone death, we are indeed truly dead already.

How apposite is this summary of mankind's predicament, skilfully hinting as it does at the contradictions inherent in human nature – the clash of light and darkness, or hope and fear in the midst of the struggle to survive and prosper at all costs. They are the opening lines of Martin Israel's very first book and they set a clear and decisive tone for the steady stream of work from his pen, which was to follow over the next thirty years.

So it was with these incisive, initial words – as perceptive and telling now as they were when they were written – that Martin embarked in 1974 upon a new career in England as a prolific and immensely popular Christian writer. He completed eventually more than twenty books in total, exploring every conceivable aspect of spirituality; the originality and depth of his thought was remarkable – the breadth of his knowledge astonishing.

Born into a prosperous Jewish family in South Africa, Martin had by this time left his youth well behind and had already passed the age of forty-five, having established a successful career as a medical doctor before adopting Christianity. Soon after publication of this first full length work of spiritual reflec-tions – entitled *Summons to Life* – he was to be received into the Anglican Church as a priest. It is a remarkable and inspiring spiritual journey, which testifies to his determined courage and profound creativity, because he had considerable obstacles to overcome in the course of his private life and public ministry.

Assiduous in his duties, Martin grew in authority and candour, even as he gained in rich diversity of experience. As his confidence grew, increasingly he came to terms with an agonising diffidence, which had mostly stemmed from acute sensitivity and shyness in his youth. Loneliness as an only child and intractable family issues at home, resulted in severe depression in later life, but the burden of this dark shadow only made him more compassionate and understanding towards those people drawn to him for spiritual direction and counselling.

His pastoral work soon extended into healing – and even into the obscure and difficult work of exorcism of evil influences, which he termed 'the ministry of deliverance' since it often required entrusting disembodied, earthbound souls into the providential care of God through rapt prayer. That Martin was able and willing to undertake such challenging and dangerous inner work extending into subtle realms beyond the gates of death says a great deal about his rare and very particular gifts of mystical intuition and psychic sensitivity, which set him apart from other Christian clergy – and marked him out as somehow different from them to say the least. Such mysterious considerations as rescue work in the afterlife hardly lend themselves to credible explanation, but Martin still wrote about these esoteric matters of the paranormal with fluent ease and matter of fact conviction.

Shy and a touch mysterious he may have sometimes seemed, but unapproachable he definitely was not. People warmed to him in increasing numbers as soon as they discovered how caring, precise and profound the spiritual direction he offered was. Before long he became sought after both as an inspired preacher and wise spiritual guide, offering retreats to both laymen and clergy. Eventually however, the unremitting demands upon his time and energy took their heavy toll. With little warning after many years of conscientious application to his ministry and acclaimed by a growing circle of avid readers as well as by an admiring church congregation, he was overcome with alarming rapidity by debilitating illness, following an acute breakdown, which occasioned a dramatic near-death experience.

He was to spend his final years mostly confined to a wheel-chair in ever-increasing disability, yet his inherent quality of radiant spirituality was now even more apparent as he flowed out in greater measure of love and wisdom to all visitors. He was indeed now living according to the sacred principles he had espoused during his ministry with such plain-speaking fervour and eloquence.

The gifted doctor turned priest had responded ardently to God's summons to sanctity, but by this point he knew more fully what such an invitation entailed, having plumbed the depths of suffering during a long and useful life dedicated in service to others.

As an eminent lecturer in pathology during his medical career, Martin was acutely aware of man's mortality, while with his deeply mystical temperament he had realised early on how very fleeting and precious life is.

And he made plain in his first book of profound spiritual instruction how tragic it is for people to waste this precious gift of mortal existence while becoming submerged in superficial preoccupations – in compensation perhaps for unacknowledged disappointment. The will to survive is natural to human beings and renders us tenacious, he said but we so easily become burdened by trivial concerns that all too often *we forget to live.* Such is humanity's central and most tragic dilemma.

The time in which we live is notable for the great scientific advances and social achievements that have swept humanity on and trans-formed its members into active units. And yet the individual is as far from true fulfilment as a person as he has ever been. What is the measure of a truly mature person? He is the one who is at home in the world because he is at home in himself.

In the mad rush for security and peace, there is too often an escape from the person to an outer world of authority, where responsibility may be laid at the door of someone else. Yet there can be no peace that does not come from the depths of our own being, no security that does not arise from the love within, and no knowledge that does not proclaim the unity of the person in the greater community of creation...

Martin showed with engaging clarity how the growth into the fullness of our own being is the awakening of a progressively greater knowledge of the being in God. Yet such knowledge is not one that is externally imposed but rather is something gradually gleaned from hard-won inner experience.

The source of personal being is at one with the fount of universal being. From the unknown streams the power behind the universe and it is in faith that we come to regard the mysterious primary cause with a sense of wonder – even while we personalise it as God – sometimes named the Author of all creation.

Such realisations lie at the heart of mystical illumination, nevertheless all verbal descriptions fall short because we cannot capture such profound understanding with any amount of striving – although earnestness of endeavour is a prerequisite for the spiritual quest. Here most certainly is an enigma to reflect upon. Reality need not be attained since it is already an accomplished fact, but it still needs to be *recognised* and then made our own if it is to mean anything.

With an open mind and heart, it is best to forget all we have learned and begin again just where we are. We approach the simple secret of our own existence most readily and become naturally convinced of God's reality as somehow not separate from our own, as we wait patiently in the stillness of attentive trust for Truth to reveal itself. This is contemplative prayer.

What appears to be a strange paradox concerning an endless struggle for fulfilment relates to our profound predicament as human beings. It revolves around the essential question of our identity and points to our pressing need for self-knowledge. It is in point of fact an acute identity crisis, which we alone can resolve.

Who are we really? Only as we begin to answer these urgent existential questions, as Martin continually reminded us, do we begin to find a truly satisfying sense of meaning. And only then do we begin to discover strength of purpose sufficient to sustain us in the face of all vicissitudes.

> *To know the true self, which alone is durable and partakes of eternal reality, requires a radical acceptance of ourselves as we really are, of the whole personality in fact. As the outer layers are recognised and put in their proper perspective, so the core or centre of the psyche is revealed. How radiant and warm it is but how few of us know it! We are deterred from this knowledge by the surrounding layers of cold and darkness. Many people strive for this central place of warmth, of which they are intuitively aware and may even have touched momentarily in meditation or during some great aesthetic experience. But few will attain its full comfort until they have made the surrounding darkness their own possession also.*

To become sufficiently determined to put into practice such a wholesome but demanding spiritual teaching is to be transformed and healed by Love. It marks the progression into a new phase of life, which is a precious opportunity for spiritual renewal. Such a task of opening up to Truth is vital work to be undertaken to the best of our ability, but a task to be accomplished patiently and with great care, because it is only after we have become reconciled to the hidden forces of darkness, disorder and negation within us that we may become a clear channel for the passage of fresh light to uplift and restore every-thing around us in the outer world.

It is ultimately only through rigorous self-knowledge that we are made fit to be of real service to the world, but this dissolution of ignorance concerning our true spiritual nature can only be managed at our own pace. We are undergoing a thorough process of inward purification and such an arduous journey through an often bare and forbidding interior landscape is seldom easy or painless. It is not in fact a task we can manage in our own strength, but fortunately when we have goodwill, Life comes to our aid in all manner of unexpected ways. We are never left without sustenance in our hour of genuine need.

Chapter 3

A Hard Road to Travel

Counselling assumes an increasing importance in the crowded, impersonal world in which we live. In the noise and bustle of the present moment, when everybody seems to be engaged in frantic activity that often bears disturbingly meagre fruits, there is more than the occasional person who seeks desperately for someone simply to listen to him. A relationship of silent attention can in itself release emotional tension, and if it is enriched by understanding words, a new perspective may be given to the distraught person so that he can proceed on his way enlightened and at peace with himself and the world.

When as a young man in the mid-1970s I first came across the teachings of Martin Israel, I was deeply troubled and badly in need of sound counselling as I struggled to adapt to life back in the West, after a long sojourn far away in India where several years earlier I had travelled in quest of Truth. I had abandoned a promising career as a journalist to 'drop out' of society acting upon what seemed to my family like a crazy whim. On my return to England, I was expected to speedily return to my senses – but things did not quite go according to plan.

I had been thoroughly shaken up and stirred deeply by a prolonged exposure to the vibrant and earthy energy of India, which is almost indescribable in its colourful intensity. The experience changed me utterly in a way I cannot easily explain. The contours of my being – the conceptions I held about myself – had been dismantled only to be sharply defined anew, but much more time would be needed for me to properly assimilate the intoxicating impressions I had imbibed.

My outlook ever since has been moulded by an alternative

view of life very different from the conventional version suggested to me by a sheltered and privileged upbringing. Deeply nourished by this immersion in Eastern culture and philosophy as I had undoubtedly been, I nevertheless felt at a loose end upon my return home and could not seem to find my bearings under the uneasy eye of my anxious father.

I still longed to be free of conventional restraints and very soon impetuously decided to travel to Scotland where I hoped to settle down away from it all. My two brothers and I had been bequeathed some money by our mother, who had sadly died from cancer when I had just come of age in 1968 – and I yearned to set down independent roots. I lost no time in purchasing a remote plot of land with my share of the legacy before embarking on a three-year course of study in the Highlands to become a nurse. I was elated to find how all obstacles had melted away and the path ahead seemed clear as day.

All went well for a while, but in my second year of study my training was abruptly cut short by a serious mental breakdown, which shattered my routine following the collapse of a love affair with another student. Before I knew what was happening I found myself rushed without delay into the admission ward of the very psychiatric hospital where I had been working as a trainee nurse. Confined to a vast, grim institution set high on a hill overlooking the highland capital of Inverness, I felt chastened and depressed. It was a rude awakening and an abrupt end to my hopes of finding a new career in the caring professions. Jubilation at my newfound freedom had been replaced by despair as I contemplated a bleak and uncertain future following the devastating collapse of all my well-laid plans.

When eventually I had been restored to health and my circumstances had improved, I came to realise that no experience – painful or otherwise – is ever wasted. That is so, provided one is prepared to heed the unspoken message it is trying to convey.

Furthermore, informed by Martin's perceptive teachings and by other equally valuable spiritual instructions I had received, I became convinced that all the events of life can be seen to fit within a foreordained pattern, determined by causes set into motion in the distant past. In other words there is no such thing as a mistake – and ultimately everything works together for good.

Naïve as it may seem, this remains my prevailing attitude – and it is one of faith regarding the essential mercy of Providence. But it is essential as one gets older to remain realistic and not slip into a state of delusion regarding that past. With the inexorable passage of the years, I have gradually gained the courage to omit less and less from what I deem to be an acceptable narrative of my life story. And as one grows in maturity, and becomes less inclined to avoid recollection of the most uncomfortable phases of prior experience, so it becomes altogether easier with benefit of hindsight to put the troubling events of life into proper perspective.

Stage by stage, as I continued on this lifelong spiritual journey with all its twists and turns figuratively speaking, I found the steep ascent levelled off – and finally I emerged on some sort of plateau where my surroundings seemed altogether more tranquil, fertile and pleasant of aspect.

Yet a pastoral image like this hardly does justice to the delicate process of inner growth. Growth into self-knowledge is mostly about trust – learning to trust the essential beneficence of the universe and the deep wisdom inherent in body and mind. The obstacles are familiar enough to everyone – crippling self-doubt, trepidation and despondency chief among them.

The spiritual path is not a straightforward ascent, but is more like a spiral with the same character-building lessons returning time and time again until they have been thoroughly mastered. Spiritual development is a long-term test of resolve and tenacity; at times it seems more like an extended ordeal by fire as one's illusions are burnt away and all that is not at peace within oneself emerges to be dealt with. The first step to freedom is often the hardest as we begin to address our deepest and most obscure fears.

We would dearly like to become established in wisdom without delay, but there are no short cuts to this kind of inward maturity. In his eloquent way and at ease with traditional Christian terminology, Martin addresses these very points with the graphic and unashamed candour so characteristic of his best written work.

All this stresses that the coming of Christ in glory in the soul is a slow process, progressive in its healing action and thorough in its capacity to change the perspective of the individual from mere self-interest to self-sacrifice on behalf of the world. We are, however, often very impatient: we look for external signs of power while averting our gaze from the revelations of inner disorder. While there is even a trace of self-seeking within us, one spark of aversion to our neighbour, the work of inner cleansing has to proceed. Furthermore, as we proceed along the inner path of purgation, so do shafts of gluttony, lust, jealousy and resentment suddenly erupt to the exterior. These embarrassments help to show us the vast distance we have to traverse before we attain a full dedication to Christ in our midst...

I had already reached the formal age of retirement by the time my own first book was published in the spring of 2013. Entitled *Hidden Beauty of the Commonplace: a nature mystic's reflections on the full meaning of freedom,* it was an autobiographical study of a sensitive writer named Clare Cameron, who had befriended me in my youth before I went to Scotland.

Clare – a lyrical nature poet at the peak of her creative powers in the pivotal decade of the 1960s – had become acquainted with many other gifted writers through her contacts as editor of a

Christian spiritual magazine. One of these authors happened to be Martin Israel – and it was in this connection that I was first introduced to his writings.

Ever solicitous for my welfare, a while later Clare introduced me to her publisher – and when he invited me to work for his firm, this had the unforeseen consequence of bringing me into personal contact with Martin too.

In the course of my editorial duties, it fell to me to compile an anthology of her work – to be entitled *Mystic of Nature* – and it immediately occurred to me that Martin would be the ideal person to provide a foreword to the new book. He kindly agreed to my request and in so doing warmly recommended Clare as bringing a *balm to the soul* and refreshment for those who are weary and depressed.

An important connection had been made – and from that moment on everything else fell easily into place. It seemed only natural then that it should be Martin also, who in May 1980 had conducted the wedding ceremony for my wife-to-be and myself at his church – Holy Trinity in Prince Consort Road – behind the grand Albert Hall in central London. It was in this step by step and distinctly fortuitous way that my destiny had become inter-twined with his – just as it had done so with Clare earlier.

As I waited in the nave of that beautiful Victorian church for the service to begin, while the guests gathered to be greeted by the quietly ascending strains of J.S.Bach's *Musical Offering* being played softly on the organ, I felt deeply moved and filled with a sense of a calm exaltation. I was keenly aware that I had reached a crucial turning-point in my thirty-two years of life and that after this definitive rite-of-passage I would never be quite the same again. I would have made the transition into a fully adult phase of responsibility as a married man and there could be no turning back to the unattached freedom of a single person.

But, in the presence of such high-minded ideals, a touch of levity could not go amiss – and it was provided by my forthright mother-in-law, who was never someone to stand on ceremony. Observing the appetising spread of refreshments laid out in the church hall following the ceremony, she could not resist bringing proceedings down to earth with a witty but rather blunt comment about the wedding cake she had made.

When during the reception she found herself standing among the guests next to Martin Israel, she impulsively dug him in the ribs with her elbow and said in confidential tones: 'I can't imagine you'll want a slice of that – now will you?'

It was a harmless enough jest, but Martin was unaccustomed to such familiarity and was taken aback. He was generally shy and awkward in social situations, but on this occasion he had no intention of keeping quiet and relinquishing his right to normal enjoyment. His indignant rejoinder was equally immediate, as he said with more than a trace of irritation words to the effect: 'What gave you that idea? I will most certainly want a proper piece of cake – why on earth not?'

I have to smile each time I recall this innocent conversational gambit, but a simple anecdote can offer a revealing glimpse of someone's essential humanity, which admits all possibilities without condemnation. Genuine humility is neither the sacred preserve of a priest nor is it to be confused with a submissive attitude in the face of inappropriate behaviour, however mild in intention. As Father Martin himself once put it – humility most certainly does not imply allowing oneself to be used as a doormat.

It was a fragment of spiritual advice that goes a long way – and I have never forgotten it.

Chapter 4

Making Sense of the Sacred

Holiness is something more than virtue: It is an attitude of complete harmlessness and love. It is a divine simplicity in which a knife-sharp discrimination is developed. This simplicity is no mere naivety – a capacity to be deceived because one's knowledge of the world is defective. It is, on the contrary, an intuitive grasp of the whole of life, informed by the undistorted action of the Holy Spirit working in the full personality – but executed in unselfconscious charity.

There is something inherently galvanizing for a writer regarding the challenge of recording another person's life properly in words. Every time I endeavour to set down reflections about someone else, I am reminded yet again of an unswerving requirement for accuracy, of the absolute need to stay true to the essential spirit of the unique human being one is striving to portray.

It is a responsibility not to be taken lightly – and I am rarely satisfied with the immediate result and often need to try again. It takes time and patience to craft an adequate description of another individual, but when you do succeed in some measure, the eventual satisfaction of good work done outweighs the difficulties of the task by far.

I use whatever device I can find to convey the essence of whatever I am trying to communicate, but spirituality is the most difficult subject of all to write about in the current climate of distrust towards religion generally and in the midst of considerable anxiety regarding fanatical religious doctrines in particular; language needs to be chosen with care in a multicultural society where insensitivity can so easily cause outrage and misunderstanding.

Ancient traditions are being swept aside and nothing is inviolable or out of bounds any more. The sacred is no longer considered beyond scrutiny or above criticism as it once was, which is not altogether a bad thing, for incalculable harm has been – and now once again is being caused – by cruel and heedless imposition of religious creed. Also science has become the new religion to be fiercely defended and championed at all costs nowadays, and scant regard is often paid for what of profound value may be swept aside in the process.

It is fully understandable that notions like sanctity and sainthood feel particularly strange and threatening to a modern, secular mentality – even so they have been indispensable in the past and in my view it is hard to justify gratuitously unrestrained mockery of religious sensibilities in the name of freedom of speech. There is surely no doubt that noble ideals still find a vital place in our busy lives today, since many of the old sacred forms of expression in worship, music and the arts had great power; without such wholesome values society would have no ethical foundation whatsoever and completely fall apart. That being the case, at such a critical juncture in human affairs, the time has definitely come to consider the real meaning and value of sacred traditions afresh without prejudice – and in the light of care and clarity.

Secular society is diminished by its suspicion of the sacred, which it does not comprehend. There is a great deal of hostility towards religion nowadays and people have naturally become thoroughly disillusioned in the shadow cast by religious fundamentalism, but this is still extremely sad because much of this disenchantment is simply due to misunderstanding.

The point is that spirituality is not the same as religion and the fact stands that the deep yearning everyone has for true meaning and purpose cannot be denied – because it is innate. When we lose touch with our spiritual origins, we lose touch with our roots – and a sense of deep insecurity follows as the true nature of reality is veiled.

* * *

Martin Israel never hesitated to talk frankly about holiness, and of its profound value in countering the darkness of worldly preoccupations. The central strand of his teaching always remained one and the same. It concerned the sacred nature of life and addressed the issue of how genuine sanctity might be best understood in contemporary terms.

As he stated in the opening quotation included at the beginning of this chapter, holiness is the expression of non-violence and pure love. But he went on to warn on that same occasion how mere virtue can all too easily become a god in its own right and so exclude the living God of love – as can even the finest of religions, to be plainly seen in the unfortunate history of the world. A holy person by contrast, Martin explained, *brings God closer to all the people he meets* – and this is accomplished spontaneously by the spiritual radiance that emanates from him.

Making sense of the sacred in today's sceptical world is not always easy. The outcome of any endeavour to do so depends on the way you begin, and originally I had considered tackling this tricky subject of holiness from several different perspectives. How might the debate be enhanced, I wondered, if I were to continue exploring now with the aid of a very different quotation from the one by Martin that had first caught my eye?

But even as I continued to delve into the question, I saw how important it was not to get caught up in words. After all holiness simply meant utter integrity or wholeness of body, mind and spirit did it not? How could there be anything complicated or contrived about the natural state of wholeness? It is near at hand and need not remain a distant prospect.

*He was very simple, very natural, and humble. As he stood at the
rostrum of the cathedral I scarcely heard what he said because of the
impact of his presence. The world outside withdrew and even the
crowd of people all about me seemed no longer there. In him was the
presence of Christ, the beauty of the truth glimpsed in one's own
mystical moments. I felt I was looking on someone very rare and
special, despite his apparent ordinariness. So unassuming in every
way, such dedicated souls are doorways to eternity...*

Holiness has its public face of course, expressed in devout
gatherings of the faithful in the presence of the great religious
leaders of the world on festive occasions, but I am much more
interested in discovering the authentic quality of sanctity, which
can reveal itself in the most surprising and homely ways.

The quotation above is a blend of these two aspects. *Doorways
to eternity* – that may seem a rather old fashioned and idealistic
description, but these few lines written not by Martin but by
another writer are still of relevance because of the effective way
they convey what radiant goodness feels like to others. It is my
contention that if you are ever fortunate enough to come into the
presence of a truly holy person, any worldly doubts as to their
veracity are likely to be wiped away in the vivid immediacy of
the moment as you are affected by this unexpected encounter in
ways you could never have foreseen.

It feels right to record by way of contrast all I can clearly
recollect of my very first meeting with another inspirational
public speaker – Martin himself. It is striking to see now how
closely my first impressions of *him* tally with the poetic account
of the previous preacher before a congregation in the lofty
surroundings of a great mediaeval cathedral; how unusual that
spiritual figure of uncertain identity must have been to make
such impact.

Witnessing the scene she describes so evocatively, was my
wise, elderly mentor, Clare Cameron who had introduced me to

Martin's spiritual teachings when she kindly loaned me a copy of his first full length book of spiritual guidance.

So near and yet so far – her portrayal of the cathedral preacher does not entirely resemble Martin, but it comes close. Her words certainly *remind* me of him and evoke his unassuming manner and spontaneous style of speaking, so fluent and free. I had not yet heard Martin preach, but I had been so much impressed as a young man by the articulate power and lucidity of his writing that I was keen to meet him and hear his message. He had a way of making everything he said or wrote compelling, simply because it was stamped without fail by the authority of deep insight and personal experience. Perhaps the following explanation by him will clarify this point:

It is no accident that people of sanctity are encompassed by an emanation of unearthly radiance which has been depicted unerringly by the great painters of the past who still had an inner eye for such details of spirituality... This radiance is the undistorted light of the Holy Spirit that pours out from a soul that is empty of guile and therefore a pure chalice of divine grace...

A soul of high stature is so transparent that the divine presence within it is fully apparent to the world: it is one with God. This state of affairs is fully applicable to Christ, but when we shed all mundane encumbrances even now and live in pure simplicity in the present moment, we too can start to become the agents – albeit unconscious of our role – of lifting up in a most amazing way all that lies around us to the very presence of God himself.

* * *

I belong to the rebellious generation growing up in the vibrant decade of the 1960s and in common with many young people at that time had become disenchanted with the staid Christian doctrine of my privileged but conventional education. As I did so, I had wandered far away from my cultural background to find inspiration in Eastern religions, and it was to take the universality of Martin's approach expressed in such sayings to attract me back to my roots.

It was the generosity of spirit and unflinching candour with which he espoused his adopted faith that made the traditional Christianity of my birth intelligible and more acceptable to me so that I was no longer estranged from my Western culture. Thus it was that I found myself making my way one Sunday morning to the large Victorian church in central London where he had recently been appointed priest-in-charge and had already earned himself a considerable reputation for his unassuming pastoral work as well as for his skill in conducting the liturgy.

I felt apprehensive and in nervous haste was much too early for the service, only to be taken by surprise when unexpectedly I encountered Martin outside the church as he was reaching into the boot of his car for things he needed before the start of proceedings. I remember how surprised I was to find him dressed in ordinary clothes wearing shirt, tie and jacket and not in the garb of a priest. He was quite normal in fact and certainly did not fit into my image of an especially holy person.

Martin was not particularly tall, but he had a keen gaze and attentive presence. He was slightly stooped giving the impression of someone studious and self-effacing yet kindly. He greeted me pleasantly with mild-mannered courtesy and to my surprise and relief I found the nervous tension of my expectations drain away as if my uneasiness had never existed. We continued to talk easily as I followed him into the dark, scented recesses of the church and then he moved softly away to begin his preparations for the service.

It was an ordinary yet quietly uplifting encounter – and it is engraved clearly on my memory as if it happened yesterday. I had not been judged – that is the point of the matter – but had been allowed naturally to be who I was with all my unspoken demands and needs. Real love is not always what we expect it to be. It works silently behind the scenes in the silent background and surprises us with its welcoming joy and ease, setting us free from the burden of the past.

Although it is clear to me that the earlier quotation, written by my friend Clare, was not an actual description of Martin Israel, it would have been quite a fitting one. This is because the evident impact of Clare Cameron's experience certainly bears witness to Jesus Christ's continuing presence of love in the world today, while Martin's healing ministry later also proved in no uncertain way to be an emphatic and enduring testimony to the far-reaching influence of love.

Clare had entitled her short essay about a remarkable preacher in the beautiful cathedral of Chichester near her home, *The Holy Man*, while Martin's book, which had made such a striking impression on me, had been given the title *Summons to Life*. It seems an appropriate choice of wording, which can be explored further. With benefit of hindsight the course of Martin's own remarkable life suggests to me that actually he had always been summoned by life to nothing less than sanctity.

For one thing he had this profound sense of vocation and for another he fully recognised he had unique healing gifts, yet how genuinely unassuming he remained. He certainly aspired to holiness and consistently expressed it in his utter integrity and wise counsel he offered to others, but as a born mystic he fully understood that sanctity is everyone's true birthright. As such holiness does not really need to be attained, but the paradox remains that it still needs to be claimed by wisdom and diligence – and seems to be mysteriously conferred by Grace. A holy person bears the precious burden of acute sensitivity to the suffering of others. The quality of holiness is a radiance seen by others for the blessing of the troubled world.

Just like Clare, who was herself a wise counsellor, Martin unobtrusively encouraged anyone who turned to him for advice to realise their full potential in recognition of the sacred nature of life. He well understood how the widespread failure to uphold the sanctity of Life is the pernicious root of all cruel and heedless actions creating disharmony and chaos. And he realised from his own personal experience of sorrow that this fundamental darkness of ignorance can only be dispelled by love.

Yet this profound love cannot be sustained without steady wisdom founded on sober insight into the basic causes of suffering. And there cannot be wisdom unless the capacity for love has been developed by moral rectitude. This is the genuine virtue, which flows from right understanding; it is not the righteous hypocrisy of the Pharisees who condemned Jesus.

The practice of virtue then is a wholesome way of living in accordance with the underlying principles of the universe – attuned to the harmonious deep rhythms of Nature. It is the indispensable foundation for a healthy and just society, less prone to all manner of social ills and the inroads of corruption. It is hardly an ideal that has been realised in our turbulent contemporary world, but nevertheless should not be dismissed out of hand, for it is the ardent hope of future generations and may yet be realised.

While remaining keenly aware of the stark dangers inherent in evangelical zeal, Martin viewed the Christian Church's ministry of healing as extending to the sanctification of the world. He never forgot however that true freedom – and healing – begins and ends with individual understanding. Only then can a community of love survive.

Chapter 5

Physician of the Soul

Out of evil much good has come to me. By keeping quiet, repressing nothing, remaining attentive and hand in hand with that, by accepting reality – taking things as they are, and not as I wanted them to be – by doing all this rare knowledge has come to me, and rare powers as well, such as I never could have imagined before...

So now I intend playing the game of life, being receptive to whatever comes to me, good and bad, sun and shadow that are forever shifting, and in this way also, accepting my own nature with its positive and negative sides. Thus everything becomes more alive to me. What a fool I was! How I tried to force everything to go according to my idea.

These simple but expressive words sent in a letter of appreciation to Carl Jung by one of his patients were indicative of a truly religious attitude on her part as well as being therapeutic, observed that great Swiss psychotherapist, adding that 'all religions are therapies for the sorrows and disorders of the soul.'

For Martin Israel, who was himself deeply moved by the contents of this personal letter quoted in Jung's writings, such a courageous affirmation of total cure clearly showed how this remarkable patient of the pioneering physician had become *a complete person in the silence of inner reflectiveness while she viewed with increasing dispassion the passing show of her own responses and the fleeting procession of the world's goods.*

She had evidently discovered the inner centre in the depths of her being – that 'secret place of the most high' – which is sometimes found at the peak of an aesthetic experience but most often revealed during a moment of *utmost dereliction*. It is only from this centre that we can arise above life's loneliness. This is *the pearl of great price* which resides *in the spirit of the soul, in the depths of the personality of each one of us.* Once this precious gem has been glimpsed from afar and claimed with diligence, *it shines radiantly within us – and from us to the world.*

As God became real to her, Martin wrote, so this courageous woman would have revealed godlike qualities in herself, especially a freed will that was able to receive and discern each new impression that impinged upon her consciousness. This new ability to remain fully aware summarized *in a nutshell* the inner work that could only be achieved by living alone for a period of time.

Such interior work in solitude, Father Martin added, was an essential preparation to render one fit for a life of higher service to the wider community. He had after all seen for himself – from harrowing, experience in the midst of utter loneliness – how resolute tenacity in the face of all obstacles has astonishing power to reveal the unquenchable flame of faith. It was a signif-icant spiritual realisation – perhaps one of the most valuable insights to accrue from long years of both inward and outer preparation for a healing ministry of his own that would require unswerving, lifelong dedication.

Eventually like Jung he would come to view his real work as amounting to the 'care of souls' – or perhaps the *cure of souls* would be a better description. In this God-given task he was to excel.

Even as a young doctor, it had become increasingly obvious to Martin that just as the disrupted rhythm of the body gives rise to physical disorders so does marked disturbance of mind and emotion cause disharmony and malaise during everyday life. It was the task of the physician to diagnose the ailment and restore order in the patient's entire domain. But such harmony is basic – *already* inherent in the physical organism on which mind and emotion depend – so the real work of intervention consists mainly of providing skilful support to the natural healing process.

Martin had further understood that the foundation of effective healing – that is to say a comprehensive cure made manifest by a changed attitude to life so that the restoration of health became durable and progressive – was *integration*. The centre of integration, he wrote was *the spirit of the soul or true self, which informs the rational mind, cleanses and purifies the emotions and renews the body with strength and vitality.*

All aspects of a human being were *under the direction of the soul, which discerns ultimate purpose in the apparently meaningless flux of everyday life, a purpose that may indeed transcend the rational barriers of life and death.*

A truly attentive doctor, awake to the spiritual dimension, is mindful not only of his patient's mind and body but also keenly aware of that person's very being. The wise physician seeks out what is essentially good in the person before him. In fact he addresses the essential being of that individual and regards him as already in unity with God as the indwelling spirit and Creator. The practitioner in this manner endeavours to kindle the flame of hope within the patient, which translates into a fresh sense of strength and purpose for him. It is this renewed purpose that paves the way for full restoration of health.

* * *

Somehow such traditional ways of practising medicine had held strong appeal for me from the very first moment I had heard about them, so it is not surprising that Martin soon came to exemplify – even as Jung must have done so for him – one of those enlightened spiritual physicians of former times.

By the time I met my own wise counsellor in Martin's guise – a physician conversant with the Jungian tradition – I had already become convinced of the natural curative power of alternative medicine, because I had seen how it takes care to preserve all that is best in medical practice from bygone days. Furthermore I had experienced its wholesome benefits while on my solitary Indian travels when over a period of four years, I had been exposed to rough and unsanitary conditions, which had seriously undermined my health and shaken my confidence in my physical and mental stamina.

As supported by the judicious use of alternative therapies, I gradually recovered full vigour on return to the West, I had already concluded for myself that the real task of a doctor was not just to cure bodily disease but to restore his patient's trust in his own innate self-worth – and kindle within him that positive sense of hope and joy to which I have referred.

I already well knew from Indian spiritual teachings how important it was to maintain a positive outlook regarding life's problems. That did not mean I had found it easy to put these beneficial instructions about surrender of self-will and acceptance into practice. Nevertheless as I persevered in my faltering attempts to face with courage the joyless moods which frequently assailed me, my inner strength grew – and as it did so I began to know the power of joy for myself.

This discovery that my life was not intended to be a burden, but could be imbued with a real sense of joy was a decisive turning point. My inner difficulties did not dissolve overnight, but at least I was on the right path. Over time – without quite knowing how or why – the firm foundation of an authentic spirituality would become established within me.

This new attitude to the challenge of living was all about the restoration of trust while learning to honour all aspects of experience no matter how unpleasant. Out of this crucible of diligent inward exploration would emerge eventually a vision of health and wholeness, gradually resolving my doubts and introducing an altogether new sense of stability.

It was a totally new beginning, but it demanded a fresh consecration of the will to the highest purpose of the quest for God and came at a price. I too would not be spared a descent into inner darkness – even as Jung's courageous patient had undergone – and I would need to access a similar depth of fortitude in order to cope with the obstacles I would encounter.

In the short term, the possibility that in due course I might become established in a faith resilient enough to withstand the buffeting of daily life was not at all apparent to me – even if the seeds of a deep interest in traditional medicine had been well and truly sown. That much was obvious as my newfound zeal as a convert to holistic medicine found enthusiastic expression in the decision to write a book on the subject. Entitled *Kindle with Joy – the task of a true physician,* it was intended to be a definitive study – and my initial Notes seemed to offer full scope for my earnest aspirations.

All too soon however it would be abruptly brought to my attention that one can hardly run before one can properly walk. In the event, this promising book about alternative medicine never came to be written. As already mentioned, the formal nurse training that I had undertaken in Scotland upon my return from India to provide me with proper qualifications for a career in the caring professions, had never been completed either as my life – so carefully assembled – fell apart without ceremony.

Indeed like countless spiritual aspirants before me, it was time for me to pass through the kind of significant rite-of-passage afforded by a full-blown identity crisis. When the stress of outer demands coincides with too much inward pressure resulting from the mysterious process of spiritual transformation, the nervous system sometimes buckles under the strain and a spell of mental instability can occur. This often results in the urgent need for the sufferer to be restrained and received into hospital care until the balance of mind is restored.

Always of a sensitive disposition and depleted by the exigencies of travel far away in India, this to my chagrin is what happened to me; evidently I still needed to learn that sometimes disappointment is the bitter medicine required to restore real health. The stubborn insistence for our personal demands to be met with a particular outcome sometimes needs to be firmly denied in order that a deeper form of healing may be accomplished in God's own good time and manner. These firm words by Martin on the subject put all this into proper perspective.

Healing is not a patchwork repair; it is the re-creation of something that has strayed from the image that God originally conceived. It follows therefore that the suffering and pain that burden the dark events of our life, such as severe illness, redundancy, bereavement or betrayal can be authentic healing agents in their own right... Sometimes we may like the Prodigal Son have to descend a considerable distance down the pit of despair before we can have the silent isolation to reflect in undisturbed clarity upon our past life. This indeed may be one reason why God sometimes says 'No' to our petitions for what we regard as healing and worldly success. Every experience in life bears its own lesson and we will not pass by the barrier it erects until we have learnt how to transcend it.

Cogent words of spiritual instruction do not come out of the blue, but find their origin in real life experience. This is what gives power to such advice, but when we forget that it consists of real words by actual human beings, it becomes remote and less potent. We are less likely then to realise the true meaning of these words in the context of our own lives. I was soon to discover that Martin Israel was thoroughly authentic in utter candour and furthermore his incisive writings always reflected his own arduous journey to wholeness. They would prove a valuable resource for years to come.

Chapter 6

Summons from Silence

Our life on earth is an invitation to partake fully of the glory of the world. This glory consists, certainly of the material riches of the earth, but there is something more in store for us. It is the discovery of the core of identity deep within us that survives the changes of the world outside us, and grows in stature even when the material world falls from us at the moment of death. We are not fully alive until we can confirm, through the experience of our life, that inner core which is our proof of purpose, meaning and destiny.

By its very nature life is of a fleeting and evanescent character and cannot be held fast. We can do our level best to avoid the lingering sense of insecurity that never seems to leave us be, yet all our efforts will be futile for 'all things must pass'. Martin Israel called this unsatisfactory but essential experience of everyday life *precarious living* – and he chose these very words to give a striking title to his second book, in which he wrote in a riveting way about his lonely upbringing in South Africa and of his own difficult path to Truth.

He started the work deliberately with a personal testimony as he felt his readers would surely demand an autobiographical sketch from someone who *dared outline the path of authentic existence,* and this luminous and succinct explanation concerning the real purpose of human life, made instant appeal to me when I originally read it as a young man in quest of self-knowledge.

Sober yet candid, his words stirred me unaccountably, for by then in my mid twenties, I had already been prompted to probe the reality of my own *core of identity* and what Martin had to say chimed with my tentative discoveries.

Distracted by troubles as I often was, I had nevertheless

already received intimations of an altogether different way of being – and these tantalising glimpses of a deeper reality beckoned me to a brighter future free of self-concern. Even so, I would not have been able to say quite why his words moved me so deeply at the time. No fewer than forty years have been needed for me to have a clearer understanding of his penetrating sayings, which never cease to amaze me with their unpretentious immediacy.

* * *

Life is fully alive – and loves to be so. Actually it knows no lack, since it is its own sufficiency and already bears within itself its own meaning. The greater life needs no reason to be and finds its joy in simply being. Our individual life is sustained by this inherent sense of meaning, but whenever we lose sight of it, suffering and confusion inevitably intervene. The stark truth of this was beginning to dawn on me.

By contrast with Martin's articulate presentation of Christian teachings, the conventional religious education of my youth had held no attraction. It seemed not only tedious, but always seemed confined in the apparent necessity of established creed. These staid biblical doctrines seemed to require huge leaps of faith, which made absolutely no sense to my inquiring mind and philosophical disposition. That is why, like so many of my generation growing up in the 1960s, as soon as I left school I had been drawn to explore Eastern religions beginning with Hinduism and a little later the Buddhism from which it arose.

As soon as I encountered Martin's quiet authority however, I sensed a striking difference in tone from any Christian teachings I had received previously. I noticed immediately how tolerant and broad-minded he was, and for the first time did not feel censored by my forays away from the Christianity of my upbringing. He fostered the mystical inclination natural to me and enabled me to discover an authentic spirituality I need not name. It was a definite invitation to make a deeper commitment to the task of genuine spiritual transformation. Here was a summons from the little known realm of silence within me that I could not ignore and there could be no going back to a mundane existence oblivious of the deep issues of life and death. It was just as Martin had described in such lyrical terms:

There is a call in the silence that leads man to the fulfilment of his life. It leads one on from the trivial round of surface living in the company of those who are travelling along a well-worn path that returns to its point of departure, and reveals a more solitary uphill path away from the crowd. It is there that the inner voice of meaning declares itself. The voice may, of course, be disregarded. It is always disturbing those who would prefer to avoid a life of deeper significance. But to those who are responsive, there is an abandonment of the world of ever-changing passions and fantasies and an entry into that timelessness of abiding reality which interpenetrates the world of form and gives it meaning.

To some people, wrote Martin, the call comes at the depths of distress or disillusionment, when through the debris of a shattered relationship or a frustrated ambition, a glimpse of a way of living more perfect than mere self-gratification is afforded. To others the summons comes like a stirring within that follows the witnessing of a deed of great self-sacrifice, or is a response inspired by eloquent words or a noble work of art. The action or the perfection of the art is an outer testimony to the eternity of life that is so often hidden beneath the blind meaningless of selfish living.

Often the call to authentic life has strongly religious overtones. It may come from the lips of a preacher or from the pages of scripture or the liturgy during an act of worship. What may before have passed unnoticed now suddenly speaks to the person's deepest need.

Virtually impossible to put adequately into words and whatever the means of awakening, it is as if a voice speaks from the depths of one's being and leads one *by a new and living way, to the life of eternity.* And that voice is of a different order from anything we know in our normal everyday experience. It is instead *the light that emanates from the deepest part of the personality, the most real point in the identity of any person, the part that is called the true self, or the soul.*

The knowledge of true being comes to us in the very place where we happen to find ourselves – *as a thief in the* night and when we are least expecting it. That is hardly surprising. After all there can be no set way, or single path to the source of this light, because each person is unique in terms of disposition, temperament, age and cultural background.

Whatever is said about God is wrong for He transcends all categories so that even a compendium of every virtue would belittle Him...

Even so it is vital we trust our own subjective experience, and for Martin the summons to a life of faith in God was not only unmistakable, but came to him very early.

He was not more than three years old when he heard, with the inward ear, a voice that seemed to address him directly in the darkness of his inner self – yet carried with it a radiant light. It gave him a preview of the pattern of his life and showed him the path he would have to follow to be an authentic person.

The path was a fearsome one. He was to pass along a dark and ever-narrowing tunnel, alone and isolated, and to move further and further away from all personal contact towards a dark, undisclosed future. There was to be no outer comfort. Lonely and often misunderstood, he would be compelled to go on in order to find and fulfil the real work of his life – even to its culmination in the darkness of death. He received the clear intimation that death was not the end, that the humiliation and suffering of a life lived in honesty were the necessary precursors of glorification. That glorification would no longer be entirely personal. It embraced all people.

Martin well understood any incredulity on the part of his readers at this precocious account of a small child's vision of his future life. But he stressed how normal his own response to it was. The vision of reality that showed him his life's work, he said, did not infuse him with self-esteem or happiness. On the contrary, he *howled at the intimation of darkness, lack of comprehension and loneliness.* The burden was almost too great to bear and yet he knew he had to persist in faith and never betray the knowledge that had been given him.

To begin with the call to authenticity he had received so early in life would lead him to withdraw from the *mass of humanity,* but the additional hardship engendered by such isolation and met with such courage would lead to an enormous strengthening of his personality.

Chapter 7

The Burden of Sensitivity

I must have been a strange child! Silence I loved more than anything else. In it I was in perpetual communion with my surroundings and with a world far greater than my physical surroundings. Each object, each flower, the sky and the atmosphere were bathed in a super-sensual radiance. Each created thing pulsated with a life that was far more intimate than the coarse, movable life of worldly activity... That there was so much dull incomprehension of the very vision of life eternal was overwhelming in its sadness for me. In the depths of receptive silence no secret remains hidden...

In just a few lyrical phrases, Martin Israel outlines how it felt growing up as a mystically aware Jewish child in affluent South Africa in the 1920s. Early on in childhood, incredible as it might seem, he had received intimation of the hard and lonely path in life he would need to traverse, but he could never communicate his prophetic vision to the adults in his world – or even to other children after he went to school.

Admirable people as they were in many respects, his parents were conventional and hardly the kind to whom he could confide his deepest thoughts. Consequently, as an only son, he had few friends of his own age with whom he could share the joys and sorrows of childhood.

To his great fortune, however, he was thrown back on the company of the African servants employed in his Johannesburg home and through their natural kindness he *did* receive the emotional sustenance he craved.

'They were simple unlettered folk,' he later wrote, 'but the unerring inner vision of a child saw in them an authenticity of character completely lacking in the Europeans I knew. In these humble servants, in their silence as well as in their joyful song, I sensed spiritual reality.'

Martin went on to describe vividly how it is in the silence that truth speaks; it requires no guile or conviviality but is completely free. In consequence these servants, who had little of their own in terms of worldly possessions, were unencumbered with pride, resentment or covetousness. They could live in the present moment, which is also the realm of eternity.

By chance it was through a servant girl that he came to understand the source of the profound spiritual vision in childhood that was to lead him along the way of solitude. Barely literate herself, she showed him a simple evangelical tract that she had been given and what he saw moved him unaccountably. Indeed it was to determine the pattern of his destiny.

This biblical tract spoke of the man called Jesus, who had loved the world sufficiently to take on its full burden of sin and who had died a terrible death for the world's redemption. As a Jew, Martin was not of a family that accepted this Christian view of salvation, but the knowledge of this man *pierced him to the marrow of his being.*

'I knew in my depths,' explained Martin, 'that it was he who had spoken to me, and that, however much I might disagree with what was said about him, I could never turn away from his life and his solemn witness to the truth... My work was to be one of reconciliation.'

Ever realistic concerning human folly, he would nevertheless always lament later how the world does not know of this mystical reality that sustains the *life of flux in which we all have to graduate to a measure of full personality.*

It was sad but hardly surprising how people so easily tended to lose sight of the embracing love that *bears up all creation in its everlasting arms* when they were immersed in surface living from day to day. And that being so it was not to be wondered at either that he himself was not understood, living as he did in a *twilight zone between mystical light that was uncreated and the darkness of material and psychical evil.*

That evil, he hastened to add, was not related to his home which, although not without shadow, was largely a place of beauty and warmth. Rather, such evil was associated with the whole created universe, which had been corrupted and desecrated by selfishness since the time of willed disobedience to the law of life, which is love for all things and for God who created them.

Mystical awareness of the fundamental unity of life brings the realisation that evil has no primary or substantive existence, but is the psychic residue left over after selfish, unredeemed action. It was important to realise, however, that evil can never simply be averted, but *must be confronted in the power of love and redeemed by love.*

'I know now as I glimpsed then as a child,' he wrote with feeling,' that He who came to me could alone redeem evil for He was love.'

When recollecting this early period of his life, Martin frequently sounded a rather desolate note, writing graphically of 'sombre progress through fear, ineptitude and foreboding' before noting the immense relief of experiencing *that light of reality which breaks forth at every moment of full consciousness.*

It was not that his own youthful existence was without joy, for he always found solace in Nature and in the intellectual and artistic studies at which he was to excel. But as an only child, what was painfully lacking was simple human contact with his peers – a lack accentuated by a paralysing shyness and social ineptitude.

His ineptitude in purely physical endeavours, such as games and creative manual work, not only made him an easy victim for bullying at school later on, but also left him with a disconcerting sense of unreality in the relationships he did have with other children. It made him strive to develop the mental side of his character, to enable him to hold his own and earn respect from those, who would have otherwise unwittingly crushed him.

How different Martin found these superficial encounters compared with the silent communion he had experienced with African servants and it later became clear to him upon reflection that he had never been properly earthed as a child; indeed it was as if his spirit had *not fully incarnated.*

'I could roam with facility in realms of mental speculation, but I doubted the efficacy of my own bodily actions,' he wrote, observing that such was the nature of the mystical temperament.

The true mystic is born not made. Someone like that had to learn to come down to earth and mix fully with all sorts and conditions of men if his life is to be successful. An aspiring mystic's task was the reverse of the much more common earth-bound man, who if he is to succeed fully, has to move beyond personal acquisitiveness to universal sympathy.

It was fortunate, Martin commented drily, that both types of people inhabit the world, for one is essential to the other – while neither is to be regarded as superior.

The fact that the mystical sense was an element inborn in a person and not just springing from their cultural background was borne out for him insofar as he had not initially drawn inspiration from spiritual books – apart from the Bible – but derived information and uplift from masterpieces of world literature.

When eventually he did turn to books about spirituality, they told him nothing new but simply confirmed what had already been revealed to him. Authentic knowledge of spiritual things, he thus felt, could never be acquired second-hand from the writings of other people, but only through first-hand experience as one lived in *receptive awareness of the contrary influences around one...* Instruction from books alone, if assimilated at all, was likely to remain merely a mental edifice soon to collapse.

Thus... *When the rains descend, the floods rise, and the winds blow and beat upon the house of intellectual knowledge, which falls down.*

Only the house built upon the rock of faith founded on spiritual experience could withstand the onslaught of the elements, as Jesus Christ taught his disciples in the Sermon on the Mount. It was this *paucity of real spiritual knowledge* that lay at the root of the failure of conventional religion to satisfy the inner hunger of modern man, Martin concluded gravely.

As this intense young man continued to grow into early adolescence, so the glory of the world's great thought and sublime music nourished him in heart and soul, but somehow he knew that this period of aesthetic fulfilment was merely an interlude – *a time of recreation before the real test began*. Even while he imbibed the wondrous beauty of life, he could not but retain, through acute psychic sensitivity, an agonising awareness of the intolerable suffering being inflicted upon his Jewish relatives through persecution by the Nazis in the far-off Baltic state of Lithuania – even as the regime perpetrated similar crimes upon countless other innocent people in Germany itself and all over Europe.

He was to discover after the war that these distant members of his own family had been burnt alive in their village synagogue in the early part of the Nazi advance into Russia; it was the kind of agonising detail the awareness of which would only serve to strengthen his empathy with the downtrodden.

The Holy Spirit works best through a well-trained, healthy mind. It is as much a duty to imbibe the beauties of life as to work in the shadow regions among the derelict, for without the knowledge of that beauty and its promise of universal redemption, there would be no message to give the derelict and broken-hearted. But my heart was broken too, even in the heights of mental stimulation and aesthetic delight, for I was in psychic contact with those who suffered, especially in the German concentration camps during the period of the Nazi regime.

Though I was thousands of miles away and therefore physically safe, an awareness of the overpowering evil that filled the world obsessed me. Through the gift of precognition, I found all too often that my worst fears were later confirmed. And yet even in this awareness of darkness and sin, there was the vital realisation that all men are members one of another, and no one who is a full person can isolate himself from injustice anywhere in the world.

Nowadays, as desperate refugees continue to flee harsh repression under the yoke of tyrannical regimes, we are taunted by the stubborn refusal of states to embrace human rights, even while we remain fixed in denial concerning the fact that all too often our own leaders have been inadvertently responsible for their emergence in the first place, due to ill-judged interference in foreign affairs.

So I cannot help but wonder how Martin would have responded to the new wave of genocides and terrorist atrocities sweeping the world. Under his spiritual direction during periods of retreat, I recall how thoroughly realistic he always was about man's immense inhumanity to man, which knows no limits or cessation.

Yet I remember clearly also how he always directed his listeners back to a clear awareness of the present moment, which never failed to bring a sense of quiet joy and relief to body, mind and soul. Stopping to be still at last, one saw plainly for oneself how it is only from this refuge of inward peace that effective actions to benefit the outer world can possibly flow.

Chapter 8

Ascent to the Light

I was borne aloft by a power that surpassed my understanding. It had no limitation but was all-pervading. Its thrust was irresistible and its action beneficent. It was the full measure of love, for with it were all things and in it life found its consummation...

The dark stillness of this eternal power was also the incomparable radiance of light, a light so intense that it illuminated the source of life and cast its heavenly rays on the meaning and communion of life. The uncreated light was the primary energy of the power of eternity, and the heavenly music of eloquent silence was its emanation into the soul.

Mystical illumination is not to be regarded merely 'as a single blinding experience of God's radiance,' Martin once emphasised, but is to be seen rather as a repeated awareness of God's love during the taxing process of inward purification, which needs to precede the supreme spiritual experience of unity with the divine.

Yet along the mystical way, there are many degrees of illumination, and some may be regarded as particularly important landmarks. It is not uncommon for a turning point of this kind to occur in the life of a mystically sensitive youngster during adolescence and this was exactly what was to happen to Martin; the profound insights he was given during this cardinal experience at the age of sixteen formed the firm foundation of the wise teachings he subsequently offered.

Even the most dramatic description or sensitive words can do little more than suggest what occurs on these momentous occasions, but an outline of the setting in which a peak experience like this takes place can be helpful in imparting the most subtle sense of the sublime and ineffable reality.

For Martin this profound opening to the light took place in his bedroom one evening after he had received disappointing results in a mathematics exam. He was considered an outstanding pupil and usually came first in the class. To do otherwise was a major disaster for him – such was his emotional vulnerability – and on this occasion he had passed although not very well. He returned home from school that day in a rather dispirited state of mind and after supper repaired to his bedroom where he settled down to listen to his radio. He knew and liked the music being played very much, but after a minute or so suddenly became aware of an alteration in his perception. The music became indistinct and the bedroom in Martin's own words became *bathed in a light of iridescent radiance...*

> *I knew that the essential part of myself, the true self or soul, was raised far above the physical body, which I could no longer see or sense; for all physical sensation had been obliterated by a new type of sensory knowledge that came not from any bodily organs, but from the soul itself... I was no longer in the universe at all, but in the realm of eternal life which is neither past nor future but only the ever-living present...*
>
> *In my situation beyond creation I could divine the onward flow of life in the cosmos... The entire created universe was shown to me symbolically as a gigantic sphere whose movement was discernible as a minute turn of a wheel, but this movement encompassed countless generations of human beings over a vast time-scale...*

As these spiritual truths were being revealed to him, Martin suddenly became aware that his own personality had been transformed and that he was no longer experiencing himself as a separate, isolated unit. Although he had not lost a sense of his own identity, he was in union with all creation and had transcended private existence. But at the moment of bliss, when unity was realised, he felt himself *being gradually but decisively lowered.*

'I was "told" with firm compassion by Him who is nameless,' Martin later wrote,'that I had had enough, and that it was now right for me to descend into the world of separation, the earth of form and aspiration, to put into practice the teaching that had been given me.'

The radiance of the light of eternity became dulled, and was soon replaced by the glow of the electric light bulb in his bedroom. Once more he was at home in bed in his physical body – *full of wonder and mute sadness* – yet still surrounded by a vibrant aura, which was gradually to diminish in intensity.

Over the next few days he was aware of *the peace that passes understanding,* but knowing only too well how little prepared his parents would be for such a disclosure, he purposely refrained from telling them about it. They would either have dismissed his experience as a dream, or else might have been seriously worried that he was *ailing physically or mentally.*

'Like the mother of Jesus, I stored all these things in my heart,' Martin noted, 'but an inner wisdom kept me from casting them before the profane gaze of the worldly ones.'

The insights that sprang from these glorious moments of revelation were abundant and priceless. Perhaps most valuable of all was the realisation of the infinite preciousness of each and every human being, for *nothing that is created is destroyed by God because of His love for all His creation.*

Death of the body is *merely a state of transition in the development of a soul-filled person,* while the way of this development is by a sequence of rebirth (known as reincarnation) with *immersion in a world of limitation to cause the soul to grow into the knowledge of love.*

Martin had learned that the power of God and the love that flows from it are bestowed equally on all creatures. No particular sect, race, colour or religious group is either favoured or exempted from that love. Above all *there is no wrath in the divine nature but only in the disregarded law that governs the world of limitation in which we have to grow to fullness of being.*

All this enlightening knowledge came to him directly with the experience – and was not deduced intellectually afterwards.

'The blinding import gave the illumination its awe-inspiring authority', Martin wrote long afterwards. He went on to observe that nothing he had subsequently read or thought had added to the content or in any way modified this remarkable revelation. The memory of it years later was *crystal clear* – and it remained the most important event of his life.

Even so he was not to be spared a further experience, which he was required to endure. This was *the dark night of the soul* – during which all spiritual light was withheld from him for many years; it was an ordeal well documented in mystical literature but little understood and he sheds useful light on its obscurity in frequent references to it throughout his writings.

Chapter 9

Saving Grace of Solitude

To admit that one is alone is the beginning of a great personal healing, to persist accepting that state of aloneness is the opening phase of a new dimension of living. To enjoy the silence of aloneness is the way to a deeper knowledge of God... When we have to bear our own company for a considerable length of time, the darkness within becomes light visible as we explore the depths of our being.

After the dramatic experience of spiritual illumination, Martin was obliged to withdraw from preoccupation with spiritual things in order to cope with the normal process of growing into adult life. This was a painful time, yet he could never forget what he had been shown and no matter how much he tried to compromise with the materialistic values that surrounded him, he could never be false to what he knew to be true.

His attention became emphatically fixed on worldly matters as he embarked on a medical career – even as his father had done prior to becoming a respected eye surgeon. Despite extreme physical diffidence and clumsiness with his hands – an outcome of the sheltered life he had led in which all menial work had been done by African servants – the sensitive only son followed his father's example by becoming adept in his own medical work and developed a real passion for the patients he met during his studies at medical school.

But Martin had not yet grown *into the stature of a man* and felt isolated, unable to make real friends with his fellow students. He was as lonely and as inhibited socially and physically when he qualified as a doctor as he was when he first went to school at the age of five. To enter a shop to buy a simple article, Martin wrote later, was *a major trial*. An invitation to a party – a rare event to be sure – would produce a state of anxiety that half paralysed his faculties for days on end.

True he was solitary by disposition. There was something of the monk about him and he always spoke of himself as a natural celibate. Yet he was to discover that this realm of solitude was close to death even as it was near to God, who is *both our friend and lover and also a devouring fire.*

Over time he would need to become intimately acquainted with this unbearable aloneness of common life. He saw how its boundaries were not set by the hour but instead extended terrifyingly into the future, without limits and without end. It seemed to *point to a life of perpetual loneliness, exclusion from the company of one's fellows and stark purposelessness.*

In the depths of aloneness, Martin observed, all one's fears are released from their abode in the darkness of the unconscious mind and they surge up into consciousness magnified by the self-centred tendencies of the as yet unredeemed personality. Nevertheless all need not be lost, for when vicissitudes are embraced by acceptance they are transformed into blessings.

Such loneliness was undoubtedly a significant factor in the depressive episodes which would always assail him, as well as a contributing element of the dark night of the soul he was obliged to endure. But it also forged an indomitable inner strength and was the source of the quiet, undemonstrative love, which was to sustain his ministry of healing and could be felt so clearly as a warm understanding by those who turned to him for spiritual guidance.

* * *

After completing his initial medical studies, Martin left South Africa in 1951 and settled in Britain for postgraduate medical training. He was aged twenty-four by then and knew that he would never return to live in his native land, for he was adamant in refusing to live in an intolerant society that practised racial discrimination under the harsh regime of apartheid.

Nevertheless when the time came for him to bid farewell to the home where he had spent his prophetic childhood, he was filled with sadness.

'That home alone knew my innermost secrets,' he later wrote as he recalled how it was there that the power and beauty of Jesus Christ had first been revealed to him with inward instruction of how he should live.

I had confided my highest aspirations to its walls and the depths of my fears were known in its rooms. In the garden I had paced out my meditations. It alone really knew me; every piece of furniture was a blessed friend.

His parents accompanied him to Europe and then after a short holiday left him to return to South Africa. The final parting was *mutely poignant* but the prospect of imminent separation must have contained for Martin an element of relief, because the relationship with his parents had been overshadowed by conflict – and the family home he had just left held dark secrets almost too agonising to recount.

He alluded to these family difficulties in the early autobiographical account of his upbringing, entitled *Precarious Living*, but it was only in a final privately-printed book entitled *Everlasting Goal* that he could bear to acknowledge openly that he had been sexually abused at the hands of his father.

In this volume Martin describes how his mother was quarrelsome and neurotic, while his father was a paedophile who 'practised fulsomely' on him.

'My mother's nature ensured I would have no friends,' he wrote, 'while my father's assault on my body degraded me so that I always felt inferior to my classmates at school.'

Such devastating mistreatment had inevitably given him an

inferiority complex and he developed for his father he admitted *a feeling of mounting hostility that eventually culminated in a healing hatred.*

He realised that many readers would be shocked by this strange description of hatred, but he was to learn that a fully acknowledged hatred could flower into real compassion and love – given genuine understanding. It was the *cold indifference* of so many relationships *masked by superficial politeness and calculated urbanity* that was truly damaging.

Though good and honest in his professional work, his father had developed a cynical attitude to the world and saw the selfish part of life as the most real, while distrusting nobility and idealism. Despite his father's abuse, Martin saw that in actual fact he as an only son *bore the seeds of inadequacy* within himself and had too strong a character and powerful a will to have been subjugated by outside influences, including those stemming from his parents

With his overriding attitude of compassion, Martin of all people would have sought to understand rather than condemn outright his father's irresponsible actions – and indeed he was able to confirm eventually that 'through the grace of God' he had forgiven his parents for their shortcomings and now remembered them with affection.

'They obviously came to me for a purpose to make me what I am,' he observed calmly. 'I can now thank them for the care they bestowed on me. I have moved in a direction they could not have anticipated… At any rate they did not stand in my way.'

Martin became convinced that much of the pain of being alone derived from having to endure inner demons such as repressed hatred of others, who are believed to be the real cause of the present loneliness. But this could be a blessing in disguise, for unpleasant as this was, it was far better for it to be exposed in full consciousness rather than remain hidden only to emerge as episodes of hatred and malice when hurt or deprived later on.

The things of darkness in ourselves have to be acknowledged clearly
as our own particular cross to bear. Only then can they be inspected
closely and dispassionately and put in their proper place.

At least the salutary experience of living alone for any considerable period of time served to show how few inner resources
one had on the surface level of existence. Even so increasing
depression at the prospect of *an unending road of loneliness* was
likely to lead to an inward crisis. This was *the moment of truth*
when one could choose life or death – transfiguration or suicide.
But at last one had arrived at *the heart of the dilemma and also to the*
way of release from it.

Now Martin had arrived in England and was obliged to fend
for himself he would have plentiful opportunity to explore those
profound principles of Truth, which later he would outline so
eloquently in his writings and which would provide unfailing
sustenance in the difficulties that lay ahead.

He was plainly set for a life of unsparing service outwardly,
but behind the scenes in private he would always need to fend
off those twin demons of loneliness and depression. Years later
he would write an assiduously detailed manual of instruction
concerning the solitary life. This book, entitled *Living Alone,* is an
astonishing text invested with the burning authority born of
stark personal experience and, as such, it may still be regarded as
an indispensable guide for anyone obliged to cope with the
austere hardship of unremitting solitude.

Yet the life alone, Martin wrote reassuringly, is not necessarily
one of isolation from the good things of the world. It need not be
a life apart from other people, a separation due to feelings of
inferiority, fear or distaste. Rather it can be a life *dedicated to the*
service of man and the development of the individual to the peak of his
excellence. In that excellence such a person can both commune
with God and be the servant of God in the world.

It was undoubtedly hard to begin with, but eventually the

things once assumed to be essential for one's life – such as the constant company of other people, society's approval, one's own reputation amongst those who amount to something in the world's eyes and the number of important people one knows – seemed suddenly to *dissolve like a mist of unreality.*

It is a revelation in those narrowed circumstances how simple life can be when it is shriven of the accretions of social usage and conformity. What at first seems almost too unbearable to confront suddenly widens out into a prospect of inner freedom, perhaps the first opportunity to be oneself since one came to self-awareness when one was a small child. It is at this point that one may begin to know oneself for the first time in one's life. The self one knows is in fact a central point within, the secret place which is the cornerstone on which the whole edifice of the person is erected.

From this secret place, Martin concluded, flowed the life of true abundance, streaming out from within and blessing the world. The person who lived from the inner centre is one from whom *the Holy Spirit pours in unremitting profusion to fertilise all those around him – not only his fellow beings but also all life.*

This was the inner meaning of the ministry of healing – one does not have to *do* anything so much as to *be* in continual communion with *That which is,* whom we know as God. And it is in accord with the scriptural dictum from St. Matthew's Gospel: *Seek ye first the kingdom of God, and his righteousness; and all these things shall be added unto you.*

Chapter 10

A New Dawn

My life in England was very different from that which I had known in South Africa. There were no servants and no parents. I was completely alone and had now, for the first time in my life, to fend for myself. I had indeed been thrown into the deep end, but was able to adapt to the changed circumstances extremely well. There was only one thing that could not be changed – my own personality.

Martin was both erudite and articulate to an exceptional degree and he was favoured with another useful gift as well. It was the keen ability to capture in just a few well-chosen words the drama of key moments along life's journey – and that is quite an art.

But in new surroundings far away from his comfortable home, he seemed to have little to fall back on except the calm and measured habits of bare necessity, for he found that his unhappy *sense of strangeness* and the inability to communicate with those around him except in intellectual matters persisted – while his social inhibitions increased in intensity.

At first he was able to absorb himself in further medical studies, but when he had achieved all he could professionally, he admitted to feeling *bereft and alone.* As usual the inability to assert himself prevented him from obtaining the level of hospital appointment commensurate with his medical knowledge, added to which he had the handicap of being an outsider with no personal backing from influential colleagues. Even so he was never out of work and was highly esteemed professionally. Considering the severe psychological difficulties under which he laboured, he felt he had made a remarkably good beginning.

During this initial period Martin sometimes lived alone in a bed-sitting room and sometimes in a hospital mess. He much preferred being in a community situation as he actually enjoyed socialising in the ordinary way, providing welcome reassurance that there was nothing wrong with him as such. It was just when some outside event like the Christmas festivities loomed large that his inhibitions mounted and he retired into a corner.

It was much the same regarding compulsory conscription into the army. He had dreaded the prospect of national service, but when soon the time came to take up his commission as an officer for two years in the medical corps overseas, he found that although he could never muster much enthusiasm for it, he valued the experience actually and learnt a great deal.

It was only after the return to civilian life that Martin's difficulties returned with a vengeance as he was thrown firmly back on his own resources. There was to be no more communal life, but only a private detached existence and he had to face his dereliction while asking himself what life was really about and what he hoped to achieve.

He had by this time become a lecturer in pathology at the Royal College of Surgeons, but it was becoming likely that he would never ascend far up the academic ladder because of his social inhibitions.

Furthermore the spiritual darkness, which had closed in on him progressively since the age of sixteen was now almost impenetrable, and he was filled with an intense and ill defined fear.

His contact with spiritual reality was tenuous, and his prayer life, which had once been a spontaneous outflow of joy to God the Creator, was now *a mere gasp in the overwhelming ocean of dark meaninglessness.*

Altogether he felt enclosed in a *fog of incomprehension.* The years were passing and yet he knew that having achieved all he could intellectually, he had in fact achieved *nothing at all.* His obsessive drive to technical perfection made his life bearable, but he felt he still had not established a real basis for living. This really was *the dark night of the soul.*

In order to appear normal Martin tried desperately hard to be sociable, but all that came of this was the unfortunate inclination to disparage or scandalise in a vain bid to be witty. When he saw what he was doing, he became ashamed and even more withdrawn for *inhibition was preferable to false conviviality – loneliness was more palatable than forced sociability.* What he did not realise then was that those around him who seemed so full of self-confidence were also suffering secretly in the midst of the politeness and polish of social ease.

The abyss of meaningless lay before everyone without exception, but apparently only he with heightened spiritual perception was plainly aware of it.

* * *

Even the most intractable situation bears within itself the seeds of its resolution. So it was that matters finally reached a head when Martin had to start lecturing to postgraduate students in a large hall. He was delighted to teach them, but was quite incapable of raising his voice sufficiently to be heard.

He visited a skilled speech therapist who quickly diagnosed the difficulty as muscular tension of the vocal cords elicited by fear and anxiety. She proceeded to teach him how to relax and breathe properly and in a remarkably short time he had overcome the vocal trouble and could speak loudly enough to be heard, even in a large lecture theatre.

It was evident, however, that the inability to raise his voice was merely a symptom of a much deeper psychological distur-bance and the therapist urged him to seek help – even as she had previously done when beset by similar emotional problems.

But Martin hesitated to do so lest any exponent of psycho-analysis he consulted attempted to brush aside his deep inner experiences of earlier years as merely episodes of wishful thinking in escape from an intolerably lonely childhood; it was that kind of dismissive agnosticism and general contempt for religious values often prevalent amongst health professionals, which he found so troubling.

'I knew with absolute certainty that those experiences had been the most real part of my life,' he wrote and added: 'If they were taken away, whatever meaning my existence held would be lost.'

What happened next was not only totally unexpected, but also turned out to be a decisive turning point, when a girl living in the same house mentioned that a psychology course was being conducted nearby. Hearing from her that she was finding the lectures helpful, Martin went along – if rather reluctantly – as he expected to receive little more than advice about emotional troubles, dryly delivered by a well-qualified psychologist replete with diplomas.

Nothing, however, could have been further than the truth. Much to his surprise, he was confronted by a stout, elderly woman, who cared little for the language of academic psychology and who had no degrees or diplomas, but spoke with loving reverence instead of the interior life and the proper inner experience of the whole person. Her entire demeanour and approach testified to the rich living wisdom of a most remarkable person; initial misgivings regarding the non-scientific basis of such 'popular psychology' were soon forgotten as the young medical practitioner was totally won over by her forthright manner.

Noting later the *curiosity mixed with trepidation* he had felt on this memorable occasion, he wrote: 'I need not have been afraid for the atmosphere of the room in which she was speaking had a calm assurance about it that I had never encountered in my professional or social life.'

The Canadian-born lecturer, named Mary Macaulay, was a courageous outsider in the psychotherapeutic field, she flowed out in a wisdom that far transcended mere intellectual brilliance – and this was because she spoke from the heart of her being, rather than from merely the head.

'I was accepted as I was – a fellow human being with gifts unique to my particular identity for the destiny in store for me,' Martin declared with evident relief.

During further lectures he attended in the months that followed, obscure themes that were buried deep in his mind but had seldom surfaced into the light of day were, to his amazement, openly discussed. They were for example profound matters like the timeless properties of the soul and the distinct possibility of rebirth in a succession of lives – reincarnation in other words. It was an Eastern philosophical concept that in its unfamiliarity still struck horror in the hearts of many Westerners – but how liberating such a message sounded in this setting.

Thus I began to unburden myself of the knowledge that lay deep within me, but which I had previously protected from the destructive gaze of the ignorantly hostile. At last sixteen years after the event, I could discuss my great mystical experience with a sympathetic person; indeed for the first time in my life I had a real conversation about the profound issues of existence.

Soon Martin met others, who had also attended this course of lectures (suitably entitled 'Understanding Ourselves'), and at last he was able to move freely amongst people with whom he could converse with ease; in this respect at least his loneliness was at an end.

His remarkable new mystical teacher soon became his friend and during this period he met several other unconventional teachers, who were healers too; each one of these remarkable individuals would in their own way have a deep influence upon his spiritual development.

Schooled as he was in orthodox allopathic medicine, Martin

had an instinctive hostility to any therapy that was not fully tractable to reason. But his dereliction and increasing humility stemming from it had made him more receptive to eccentric approaches to the spiritual life.

The essence of healing, he concluded, is catholicity – it is an all-embracing sympathy, which rejects nothing of help wherever it may come. This is truly what it means to be holistic.

Martin as a mystic was naturally sympathetic to all the great world religions, and Eastern philosophy in particular earned his glad approval. But soon he was to embark in addition upon a comprehensive tour of every other spiritual teaching under the sun – plus the full range of alternative therapies as well – bringing to bear upon each approach his kindly gaze but ferocious intellectual discernment.

'It seems that I was taken under the auspices of the Holy Spirit to these various outposts of the occult in order to understand their attractions and to discern their over-all inadequacy in fostering true spirituality,' he explained.

That was not enough, however. It was not long before he was induced to quit the role of interested observer of complementary therapies and himself start practising healing by the laying-on of hands.

Indeed Martin soon found that, under the influence of these new unconventional friends, he had been *given his marching orders* as a healer putting a rapid end to his indecision. Upon reflection later he must have wondered whether his decision to obey had been wise, for he regarded his introduction into the healing ministry as *decidedly suspect*, while his earliest associates were, to say the least, extremely eccentric in their belief systems.

'But one learns to plough one's own furrow as experience opens one's mind to new revelations of the Holy Spirit,' he acknowledged in his matter of fact way. There was no other field of human endeavour that laid bare one's inner nature with all its weaknesses so clearly as the healing ministry – yet it was also an endeavour that *fulfils the innate nobility of human nature as it aspires painfully to the vision of God.* Years later he still recalled to his amusement how unprofessional he felt as he made his first attempt to practise contact healing.

'To assure myself that I was not really a charlatan, I resolved never to charge anything for my service, a resolve I have mercifully been able to fulfil to this day,' he wrote.

Martin proceeded to hire a small suite of rooms in a poor state of repair and applied himself to the physical task of painting and renovating them, which he considered was a remarkable achievement for him. At long last the consulting rooms were ready for use – and the first of many patients arrived.

He was to witness dramatic improvements after treatments sometimes that caused him to 'raise his medical eyebrows', but he wisely refrained from final judgement – well aware as a doctor of the vagaries of chronic disease. Instead, in each case, he entrusted the final outcome to God and never failed to conclude a healing session without sharing with his patient a period of quiet prayer in thanksgiving.

Chapter 11

No Turning Back

Once God and the transcendent are eliminated from man's range of thought, and man himself becomes the measure of all things, aspiration fails, and people become mere chattels in the hands of their more unscrupulous fellows. The Church is the repository of divine revelation; even if it has often betrayed its custodianship, it has always been sustained by the blessed company of saints and martyrs.

If faith is to be fit for purpose and able to withstand the toughest demands of everyday life, it needs to be forged in the fierce heat of authentic experience, and tempered by lessons of trial and error well heeded. Once this has been accomplished, life is never quite as painful again; our joys are set free to become immeasurably deep, while our sorrows – grievous though they may still be – are altogether easier to bear.

A deep sense of faith, even if it cannot be clearly articulated, gives rise to fresh hope and trust that somehow we are now being sustained by a higher power and that somehow everything will work out for the best. Martin must have rejoiced in just such a feeling of exaltation as the persistent mood of inner darkness finally lifted and spiritual light was restored to him.

But as his inner vision cleared, while his unstinting investigations into diverse aspects of spirituality continued, it became increasingly evident to him that he *would never find a home in this confused mass of esoteric thought* to be found circling around the perimeter of the great world religions – even if such fringe teachings were certainly not without merit.

More and more Martin's mind turned instead towards contemplating the merciful figure of Christ, who had disclosed

Himself to the young Jew in a full measure of Grace when he was *scarcely out of infancy*. Ever since then there had been no escape from Jesus even if he had been so inclined, for he began to see Him *as the consummation of all that Judaism had taught and witnessed and also the power of God universalised to all men, of all races.*

He had long considered himself something of an outsider with an intense young man's rather radical political, social and metaphysical views. He had for this reason held back from institutional religion lest he should lose his spiritual freedom within the close confines of dogmatic sectarian creeds. But despite himself he found that his fixed outlook was beginning to shift as he became more sympathetic to the established Church.

Not that he had any illusions about Christianity, for as a child in South Africa he had met enough Christians to see that their religion did not 'appear to bear any great impress of holiness'. However, he now saw the Church, despite its failings and past episodes of 'persecution, cruelty, obscuration and fanaticism' as the *ultimate bulwark against barbarism* and also that constant carping criticism was unhelpful of change.

How much finer it would be, he thought, to join and help from within rather than criticise from outside where one was 'both impregnable and useless'. It was becoming evident that in his words he was being *impelled* by the Holy Spirit to active Church membership – and in so doing he would find to his relief that he would have to surrender none of his previous metaphysical views; on the contrary he would return to them anew to find them strengthened and confirmed by a deeper understanding of the Bible and the early Fathers of the Church.

During this crucial period of Martin's life, there were some further significant developments, which would have considerable bearing in moulding his new outlook. For one thing he had discovered to his surprise after successful speech therapy that he had an inspirational gift for public speaking; it was spontaneous spiritual utterance of *such a calibre*, he noted, that he was soon able to deliver completely unprepared addresses and lectures lasting up to an hour.

'When I reached the silence and lifted up my soul to God in prayer,' he wrote, 'His Holy Spirit descended on me, and I started to speak with an authority and elegance far outside my usual range.'

He could not help but notice with interest how it was that a weak voice had led to his *final liberation*, yet that same voice, now firm and assured, was to be *the principle means of liberating others from the shackles of meaninglessness and fear.* Later the pen was to *supplement the spoken word,* so that the message could go out further afield.

Martin had begun giving talks by now on spiritual and psychological topics and was encouraged to find them increasingly well received, first by audiences interested in esoteric teachings and before long more by churchgoers and clergy in the Anglican tradition. As someone previously suspicious of organised religion, it was a matter of delight that his somewhat unorthodox approach to spirituality was proving fully acceptable to mainstream Christians, showing how much more liberal the Church had become since the more rigid religious climate prevailing in the days of his youth.

'My theme was the abundance of life – both on earth and in eternity – that a full understanding of Christ can give man,' he wrote and added ardently: 'However much I tried to be detached in my psychological thinking, I could never remain long without mentioning Christ, in whom the fullness of the Godhead dwelt bodily, as a presage of the day when the remainder of mankind would also partake fully of the divine nature that was at present lying dormant within it.'

This joyous theme filled him *with spiritual radiance* as he proclaimed it, and his audience responded with warm appreciation. Soon Martin was invited to conduct spiritual retreats –

tranquil occasions that provided the ideal environment for him to communicate his message in depth. Retreats in a conducive, natural setting would in fact become his favourite form of teaching by far. He would always speak highly of their great value in establishing for people of all ages and from all walks of life the firm foundation of a life of prayer as they took the welcome opportunity to reflect upon their lives well away from the clamour of the world.

In all manner of ways the summons to serve God in a definite role was becoming more insistent by the day – and such an incisive call to make a clear commitment to do so could hardly be ignored. Presently a heartfelt pledge would be made, the die would be cast and then there could be no turning back.

* * *

When all goes well and obstacles melt away unexpectedly, it sometimes seems as if the universe itself is offering its tacit approval of our dearest hopes and plans. Certainly Fortune appeared to smile in this manner on Martin the day in September 1975 when he was finally received into the priesthood of the English Anglican Church – filled perhaps with the quiet sense of gladness of someone witness to their appointed destiny.

That simple ceremony in the City of London church of St. Michael's, Cornhill was the culmination of years of intense inward preparation – and yet the medical doctor turned priest had not undertaken formal theological training. A notable exception had been made in Martin's case, and the usual stipulations waived, as he had effectively been fast-tracked into the ministry on the basis of his evident grasp of biblical doctrine and increasingly assured reputation as an inspired lay preacher and assiduous conductor of spiritual retreats.

A wonderful description survives of this special occasion, which affords us a vivid snapshot of an absolutely key moment at the very beginning of his far-reaching healing ministry. In a quietly amused letter written by a friend who was there, we learn how the small church usually had a congregation of just a dozen, but on that Sunday it was packed to the doors.

There were no less than three bishops and other senior clergy present not to mention any number of psychiatrists, marriage guidance counsellors and numerous other figures from the caring professions packing the pews. The ceremony was at once *impressive and simple*, while Martin himself – the only one being ordained – looked *shy and thoughtful... a little solemn like a grown-up choirboy* – and *absolutely radiant* as he was led down the chancel by the Bishop of London.

If one considered the Christian Church a family, wrote his friend, this was just like a family occasion – *natural and not at all pompous; the atmosphere in the church was perfectly lovely.*

It was already clearly evident from the enthusiastic gathering how, despite his shy demeanour, Martin had the rare ability to empathise deeply with many people so enabling him to meet their unspoken needs but in a most unobtrusive way. Such responsiveness evoked great affection and loyalty from those whom he counselled, and this special psychic ability was one of the gifts of the spirit, which was to render him such a trustworthy spiritual guide.

So too, it is said – but from quite a different perspective – that the existing incumbent of St. Michael's Church, under whom Martin was to serve as an unpaid curate for three years, was *a little startled* to find *all manner of folk* approaching his newly ordained assistant for deep spiritual counsel.

Martin's personality was an intriguing blend of exceptional candour, unassuming reticence and insistent privacy, kept for the most part in admirable balance. Despite the fact that he was not consistently forthcoming, his writings are so extensive that it is quite possible to construct a coherent narrative of his life story from his own observations of a personal nature. Inevitably, however, frequent gaps still remain – and these pose a problem for any aspiring biographer.

Just when I needed them, I found further fascinating details in an excellent commemorative book, which was published in tribute to Martin Israel some six years after his death, at the age of eighty in October 2007. This slim but substantive volume (entitled *Martin Israel – An Appreciation*), contains the essence of his teachings with full details of the many books he wrote, but also includes numerous colourful anecdotes from his admirers along with moving accounts of their varied spiritual experiences under his guidance.

With a sense of gratitude to the contributors and publisher, I have not hesitated to draw upon these contributions to elaborate upon certain points I wish to make, or describe more accurately important turning points upon Martin's own life's journey – such as that highly significant day of celebration when he became a priest and properly embarked upon his healing mission.

Chapter 12

The Supreme Privilege

In our small portion of the mighty cosmos it is a privilege to be born human, for we are thereby given the power to know God in conscious recognition, to work with him and to penetrate the most intimate secrets of the creation. We can think the thoughts of God, but also have the power to use that knowledge selfishly for what we short-sightedly believe to be our own interests – or else we can give that knowledge to the world for its greater blessing.

Martin's writings are quite unforgettable, potent in terms of both clarity and insight. His words penetrate to the very heart of the Christian mystery, peeling off layer upon layer of symbolism to reveal the shining essence beneath – and showing furthermore how profoundly relevant these traditional religious teachings of Christianity remain in our troubled contemporary world.

But there is a high price to be paid for the wisdom of deep understanding and Martin counted the cost at times in a bitter harvest of suffering to be endured in the form of debilitating physical illness and recurrent psychological depression. He viewed such vicissitudes as inseparable from the path of growth into full humanity and took care not to become embittered, teaching by his own example how the inevitable challenges of life are not to be resisted or resented but welcomed with fortitude.

In this manner adversity is made more bearable – and even the inimical influence of an adversary may be utilised and transformed into blessing. And Martin went further still in a daring interpretation of Christian doctrine, suggesting that almighty God – the author alike of prosperity and trouble as the primary source of all things – actually allows the emergence of evil as part of His *magnanimity*.

This was indeed a curious word to use in connection with demonic destructive forces, he admitted, but without their stark impingement on the psyche of all evolving creatures, there could be no real progress.

It was an idea – startling in its originality and conceived following a personal crisis – that helped pave the way for another book, perhaps the most impassioned yet. Entitled *Coming in Glory*, this new work encompassed the theme of Christ's advent in the universe and His continuing active presence in the disturbed world of today.

The second coming has long been awaited by Christian believers, but in reality Christ has been coming since the start of creation, Martin wrote. This cosmic Christ found his glorious summation in the person of Jesus of Nazareth, but His final appearance depends as much on our own receptivity as on the inscrutable will of God.

He is with us fully when we are fully human; the task of humanity is the lifting up of all creation to a knowledge of God, the raising up of the dead to new life.

When we are ready, when we have given up ourselves fully to God's service and have sacrificed ourselves for the good of all, a new life will come to us also, and we will see him as he really is. And so the Word at the beginning shows himself as the Word made flesh. When that Word is deeply incarnate in all humanity, we will be changed and see him as he is, the Word triumphant.

Christ has died:
Christ is risen:
Christ will come again:

This stirring acclamation, which Martin was moved to include in the Prologue to the book he was beginning to write, stands out as the most glorious affirmation of Christian faith. But in this context it also perhaps served to convey his own tremendous sense of relief as he suddenly emerged from the deepest spell of depression he had ever experienced, and into which he had been plunged while convalescing from a serious illness, which had afflicted him just nine years after his ordination.

It seems that he had suffered a fall, which had damaged his arm and shoulder, necessitating an operation plus a stay in hospital. It was during the extended period of convalescence, while being cared for by a kindly, elderly parishioner that a crippling sense of despondency overwhelmed him.

During this troubling period Martin had felt completely cut off from his usual source of creativity, while prayer – normally regarded by him as 'the staple of his life' – could only be conducted by rote, for he was encompassed in a darkness that resembled a 'pea-soup type of thick fog'. At the same time he was flooded by emotional memories and overwhelmed by mental pain almost too acute to bear.

Despite this, as he continued in intercessory prayer, all at once there was a significant change in his inward perception. He suddenly became aware of a blue light on his spiritual horizon as had been usual in the past while engaged in prayer during his healing ministry. This was the first sign that at last he was on the road to recovery – and could perceive something of the spiritual realm once again.

Martin then described how, soon after this crucial experience of God's grace, he had been granted *an inner vision of the redemptive work of Christ in the individual soul.*

'I was shown', he explained, 'that the darkness symbolised a radical purgation of the inner life of all that was egoistical, so that freed of all mundane dross, the soul could now be the repository of the light of God...'

'I realised how imperfect had been the list of my priorities in the past, how I had concerned myself with such ephemeral matters as status and income when my life should have been

dedicated entirely to God and my fellow creatures, how providential had been my severe illness. I had been saved by my
continued practice of prayer when all seemed futile. Then Christ
had in truth been born in my soul, and a new conception of his
incarnation in the entire cosmos had been vouchsafed me.'

This conception was grand in scope and would be set out in
minute and articulate detail in the book he was about to write.
Following this liberating vision, he was inspired to scale new
heights of superbly constructed thought; as ever his insights are
profound, his modes of description evocative and his delivery
powerful and assured.

Never had Christian doctrine and biblical lore made so much
sense to me as it did after reading Martin's masterly account of
the manner in which Jesus Christ remains very much alive today
in the twenty-first century. At last I too – born into the Christian
faith but long an outsider regarding its theological convictions –
could perceive clearly how Christ's merciful light shines on in
the dark shadows of our contemporary world. In the past I had
regarded the notion of the second coming as far-fetched and
fantastical, but now I was beginning to discern in what
undeniable fashion it is actually coming to pass.

Chapter 13

Sparks of Fire

And so the light of God which is the life of men shines on in the darkness of human ignorance, and an inextinguishable spark illuminates the way of even the most intransigent creature. The life-giving wisdom of the Word may be spurned amid the meretricious glitter of the attractions of the world, but a spark of divinity lies in the depth, or ground, of the soul. It does not consent to sin for its nature is divine...

Now in an elevated mood of renewed hope following his vision of Christ's redemptive work both in the outer world and within the inward depths of his mind, lucid insights seemed to flow forth from Martin like a bright, running stream.

Through the finely focussed prism of his new book, he was able to describe in his most informative and assured style – distinctive enough to engage the most disinterested of readers – how God's supreme gift to all his creatures is the knowledge of himself that he has implanted in them. For we all bear in our inmost soul *the very stamp of God's being... the effulgence of the divine splendour* which is no less than... *the sustainer of the entire universe.*

God's most profound love for us, Martin ventured to explain, represents a gracious invitation as well as a directive towards the fulfilment of life, but crucially we also have been granted freedom of choice, which is the power to collaborate with the divine source or set ourselves up in competition with it. This is the way of *selfish advancement* – and inevitably it brings suffering to our door as Adam and Eve discovered to their shame and chagrin when they were cast out of the Garden of Eden in the creation story of the third biblical chapter of Genesis.

In establishing their own separate identity, our two unfortunate primeval ancestors sacrificed their intimate knowledge of God, and this exclusion from the divine source through the selfish exercise of their free will brought with it impermanence and death – for life resides only in the power of the Holy Spirit, unimpeded by grasping self-concern.

As materialistic self-interest grows, so does the knowledge of the Word – the understanding of the overall purpose of existence – recede until it is completely overshadowed and occluded by the impenetrable darkness of incomprehension and meaninglessness. Life now assumes the character of a series of apparently unrelated events that punctuate time until decay and death close the scene.

So this is how the fundamental sense of separation from the essential unity of life comes to pass, and the nagging pain of alienation which follows in its wake is largely responsible for the incessant sorrow and strife afflicting human beings. It is indeed a vast pit of suffering, which words of fable or analogy can never adequately represent, and Martin must have seen this tragic situation with absolute clarity the moment the sombre darkness of his depression lifted and spiritual light was restored to him.

In the recalcitrant lower depths of human nature, there is plainly so much that is selfish, unclean and destructive, he observed, yet the drama of conscious existence lay precisely in this *constant interplay within it of darkness and light, of shadow and substance, of reflection and reality.*

It was evident to him too that the darkness dare not allow the radiant light, in which it has its true being to touch and transform it, preferring *a subterranean, lurking existence to full exposure where healing and transfiguration could follow.* How strange that this darkness would seem to abhor the very light from which it has emerged, but *the darkness that is the antithesis of the light of God is also its complement, for in the final analysis every living form and every emotional power has its origin in the one Father that is the creator of all that is seen and unseen.*

This spark of God, which sustains every living creature without exception is *inextinguishable,* as Martin indicated in the opening words to this chapter. Furthermore not only is this essential gleam of goodness man's saving grace but also it provides without fail *a source of growth, maturation and fulfilment –* provided that the still, small voice of conscience proceeding from it is heeded.

The golden rule of all spiritual teaching is summarised in a single sentence: do to others as you would have them do to you. The spark of God – his Word which brings knowledge of the presence and nature of the Godhead – lies revealed every time we chose the path of unselfish sacrifice in matters small or great.

The smallest gesture of goodwill – this conscious commitment to bring love into the world – fills us with a joy *that exceeds personal aggrandizement.* And in this way the seed of the Word *germinates into this present life, assuming the initiatory role of mentor into the deep secrets of eternity translated into the current world where we find ourselves.*

In every generation, wrote Martin, there are those few who have grown beyond the attachment to possessions and the distorted view the world has of success and wealth to *a vision of wholeness that includes all creatures while lifting them up to the source whom we call God. In these few, the seed has attained the stature of a tree – the veritable tree of life – and under its boughs the compatriots of the spiritual master will find shelter and nourishment.*

Our conscience is a quiet expression of the voice of God within us that nevertheless *speaks with prophetic authority;* it is *the apex of the mountain of conscience, an incontrovertible focus of inner judgement within each of us that is disregarded at our peril. Only when it is acknowledged and accepted can the great work of transmutation be started.*

The glory of the fully realised human being, Martin concluded, lies in *his conscious self-giving to God at the moment in hand. When he has lost himself in service to his fellow creatures, he has found his true nature, his authentic self in God. At that point in time he moves beyond the form of a circumscribed individual and attains an identity that embraces the total human consciousness.*

* * *

Martin was solitary and studious by nature, but he was also generous in communication and draws readers without reserve into the profoundly rewarding world of his inner reflections. Nevertheless, in order to fully appreciate the subtleties of his more abstruse ideas, it is at times necessary to withdraw from the closely argued development of his thought in order to find a different kind of refreshment in the elegant simplicity of the original biblical sources from which he had drawn.

He had chosen to base the beginning of his powerful present volume about the second coming of Christ upon the much loved verses of the Gospel according to St. John in the biblical New Testament – a prologue, which he found *incomparably majestic.*

When all things began, the Word already was. The Word dwelt with God and what God was, the Word was. The Word, then, was with God at the beginning, and through him all things came to be; no single thing was created without him. All that came to be was alive with his life, and that life was the life of men. The light shines on in the dark and the darkness has never mastered it.

The verses of the Fourth Gospel that follow are no less beautiful in their dramatic intensity as they describe the striking figure of John the Baptist, who has been sent by God to foretell the healing ministry of Jesus:

There appeared a man named John sent from God; he came as a witness to testify to the light that all might become believers through him. He was not himself the light; he came to bear witness to the light. The real light that enlightens every man was even then coming into the world.

That real light, Martin pointed out, had in fact been *performing his enlightening work from the dawn of creation, so that the indomitable human spirit could sweep aside all obstacles from its path in its onward thrust towards the mastery and reclamation of the world.*

And now the same pure light was *attaining full incarnation in one whose soul and mind were so transparent that the divine energy could show itself at time and point of space by effecting a transformation of the coarse psychic atmosphere surrounding the life of this world... The end of this psychic transfiguration was a universal heightened compassion that embraced all human existence, being no longer foreign to any sordid detail of mundane degradation.*

The end of the life of Jesus – embodying God's Word on earth – represented a willing submission to the forces of darkness. In making the ultimate sacrifice, Christ was now assuming the burden of the sins of the world.

Though without sin himself, so that there is no cloud of impurity to come between his soul... and God the Father, he voluntarily enters the scarcely penetrable fog of psychic evil and starts to clear it.

The raising up of all creation to God that resulted from this act of supreme sacrifice, concluded Martin, is the eternal significance of the ministry, passion and resurrection of Jesus described so movingly in the Fourth Gospel of St. John.

Chapter 14

Healed by Love

The darkness that is healed by love has a peculiar contribution to make to our common good in that it can in turn approach the raging agony of life and bring it to the peace of acceptance. Only that which has known the powerful forces of destruction, submitted to them in abject faith, undergone disintegration, and then experienced regeneration, can be a worthy companion to all who suffer and are in raging torment.

Martin here sets our own often humdrum but still sometimes agonising mortal experience against the supreme example of self-sacrifice set by Jesus Christ, whose earthly life ended *enveloped in the gloom of doubt and astringency of failure.*

For all Christians this is an essential link to make, but it takes a good religious teacher, who is lucid and skilled in theological exposition, to bring out the true relevance of this striking contrast between the ordinary and sublime, which is so often taken for granted in a routine profession of faith; only then does the familiar biblical narrative cease to be stale and become enlivened by a fresh sense of meaning.

Not only is the scriptural interpretation that Martin gives of these momentous events in his writings bold and sometimes enthralling, but with quiet clarity he always manages to instil calm and alleviate confusion. It was in this remarkable way that he would meet the sceptical gaze of a complex, contemporary world with the steady assurance of firm convictions, which in his sermons were conveyed in a steady stream of words that seemed to flow spontaneously from him to transform the rapt listener.

It cannot be easy to unravel the tangled misconceptions of a youthful mind that have been carried into adulthood, but this was the challenge to Martin's communication skills that my own disenchantment with Christianity represented. Fortunately he was a good pastor to his scattered flock and his parishioners were in safe hands. In his kindly, non-critical way, he encouraged errant sheep back to the fold, but you hardly realised he was doing so – such was his unassuming manner.

* * *

The quotation from Martin Israel that begins this chapter points to a fact, which is challenging and liberating in equal measure. When through suffering, we come to know we are helpless if left to ourselves and nevertheless experience true love in the midst of desolation, we can at last admit that love is undeniably real and grow as people in its radiant warmth.

It is mysterious how it does so, but pure love has to assimilate the darkness of the world around it, confronting the baseness of so much human nature in order to accommodate the demonic element of life. Only then can the darkness be lifted up to the light and its powerful negative charge make a positive and powerful contribution to the growth of mankind. This was the supreme mission embraced by Jesus, but it is also our task and responsibility. To the degree that we can acknowledge and accept what in truth is a sacred duty, to that measure are we set free to live life to the full.

Having indicated these things, Martin proceeds to describe in the most graphic and realistic manner, the menacing atmosphere of *naked evil and despair* which must have prevailed in the garden of Gethsemane at the time of Christ's betrayal; this was the dramatic scene which preceded the *ignominy of public disgrace with its attendant malice* on the cross of Calvary.

It was important to grasp, he wrote, how far Jesus was from understanding the full import of his ministry and passion during the last part of his agony on the cross. At this critical moment not only did God the Father seem to have forsaken him, but the validity, let alone the success, of his mission was sorely in doubt as the forces of darkness *hemmed him in to the point of suffocation.* It was only when he died that his full glory would be realised – and it was the Roman soldiers guarding him who were the first to be greatly moved by his noble bearing and calm acceptance.

The darkness that Adam and Eve had originally brought upon themselves as an inevitable part of their growth into self-knowledge according to the Genesis story, Martin explained, was now in the great event of Jesus' resurrection to be brought into *the full light of another day,* so that it could be finally delivered from the realm of evil.

The *spark of divinity* that lies eternally in the holiest part of the human soul had at last finally been cleared of the usual surrounding miasma of sin and could shine as *an inextinguishable beacon* in the world. As the physical body of Jesus was changed into spiritual light, so the whole created universe was given its first glimpse of the total resurrection of matter to spiritual essence. But before this could be accomplished, there had to be the resurrection of human nature made manifest by the healing power of Jesus to be received by all who could accept it.

It was a transformation initiated by Christ in historical terms long ago, yet it has had a distinct and uneven momentum all of its own – and this is the burden of incarnate life, which we all continue to share. From a Christian perspective it is in fact the very basis of the world's amazingly creative but turbulent history.

By undergoing physical crucifixion, Jesus established the primacy of love and showed that the nobility of the spirit could never be eclipsed by terrible suffering or even death. This was the dispensation of the New Testament – the essence of the Christian Gospel. Far beyond any conflicting words of theological dispute, the resurrection of Christ can be viewed as becoming a reality howsoever it is interpreted – for *survival of death can be known only in our life through the power of love...*

Our existence is a by-product of the divine love and our immortality is a manifestation of that caring, which will never cease to provide for us no matter how much we may reject it.

* * *

In this single world we inhabit in all its troubled beauty, the quality of our own experience depends on the state of our consciousness. When Christ was with the people of his time, his very presence heightened the awareness of all who were open to him. From the usual *earthbound preoccupation* with *undertones of selfish isolation,* his contemporaries *were raised to a world-embracing response that included all created things.*

It was interesting to study the change in perspective that the life of Jesus wrought on his disciples, reflected Martin. They had been summoned from their earthly trades to follow him, and their call was to be 'fishers of men', but first they had to be *cleansed of all mundane dross and freed from materialistic illusion.*

How wonderful it must have been to claim membership in that exclusive yet unobtrusive fellowship, to be the constant companion of the lord of life from whom emanated in a pure fountain of radiance the Spirit of God? In his presence all the answers to life's problems seemed to be available, while failure was not so much to be envisaged...

They believed they had attained spiritual mastery. And then the centre of their hopes, the focus of their lives and the meaning of existence itself, suddenly appeared to fail. Jesus was led into the hands of sinners who had him condemned to death...

Abruptly the disciples had to learn the hard way *that failure is the glorious crown of worldly success, that pain lies at the heart of the healing ministry, that death puts an end to earthly life in order to set in motion a true resurrection of the personality. None of the spiritual truths is to be understood by the unaided intellect; each is approached and made intelligible by experience in which the lesser certainty is sacrificed in faith for the greater hope dimly displayed before us but beyond rational conception.*

We have become thoroughly accustomed to the traditional account of Christ's passion, but how essential it is to remain alert to any intimations of deeper meaning that may flow from our own reflections upon it. The crucifixion and resurrection are momentous events intrinsic to the Christian mystery. Naturally they evoke a sense of awe and wonder, but any interpretation of their significance still needs to remain relevant and credible to the modern mind if it is to claim serious attention and remain adequate to mankind's most dire requirements.

We live in a period of immense possibilities, but great turbulence, which seems destined to be continually framed by sorrow. At such a hazardous time, doubts in particular are a valuable feature of a tentative growth in faith. Never to be ignored or evaded, they are best met face on, since it is then that we can make the most valuable discovery of all – that our deepest doubts are the source of our greatest nourishment and most enduring hope.

Perhaps such observations may accord with the drastic fluctuations in mood endured by the disciples after Christ had been abruptly taken from their midst in the brutal finality of death. It must have been a period of agonising uncertainty followed by dawning hope as their beloved Master unexpectedly returned and moved among them in his resurrected form.

During those forty days during which time Jesus appeared to his disciples, Martin related how *their amazement must have blossomed into the bliss of recognition, the relief of purpose ending a grey period of disillusionment of waning hope after so great a promise of glory.*

Afterwards Christ's Ascension would be followed ten days

later by the descent of the Holy Spirit on the assembled body of believers. Christ was now no longer available as a person, *but was universally present as the Lord of life.*

So it was after the pentecostal experience, concluded Martin, that *the band of rather faint-hearted apostles was cemented into a fellowship that faced constant danger and death with impunity.* Now they knew once and for all for themselves that *even if the body was destroyed, their life in the risen Christ was assured.*

Chapter 15

In the Footsteps of the Faithful

Those who call on the name of Christ in fervour and dedication are by that very devotion lifted to his presence, and a new world opens for them. Thus they have attained a knowledge of the Kingdom of God at that moment, which is the point of intersection of time and eternity.

But, alas, that supreme awareness is evanescent, and almost at once we relapse into the divisive atmosphere of our mundane environment and become imprisoned in a mass of destructive thoughts and attitudes. These impinge on us from the indifferent surroundings where we perform our daily work, but also from the unplumbed depths of our unconscious lives where cesspits of hatred, resentments and lust lie exposed to the general atmosphere of doubt, selfishness and purposelessness that surrounds the world.

How unashamedly indelicate if not profane these final lines from the above passage would sound coming from the pen of any religious writer of conventional persuasion – but then Martin Israel was anything but conventional. Anybody who got to know him well soon discovered that this was one of the most delightful and intriguing things about him: That such a shy and mild mannered man should be capable of such a written response, impassioned and quite unabashed in tone, was a good reason for admiration.

Cesspits of hatred, resentments and lust – it was hardly the kind of language you would expect a well-respected priest to deploy. But as a seasoned contemplative himself, Martin well understood how beguiling were the temptations and probing the challenges likely to be encountered by anyone wholeheartedly embracing a life of authentic spirituality and he wanted to make this abundantly clear.

At least in our own lifelong pursuit of wisdom, we can count on the implicit support of not only unconventional teachers like Martin but also the blessed company of the faithful down the ages, who have already undergone the vicissitudes pertaining to spiritual growth and emerged unscathed and whole in integrity.

Of course in their own day these so-called 'faithful' were often regarded with stern disfavour by intolerant religious authorities, who condemned them as heretics and harshly punished them with death and worse; in point of fact these outsiders were simply courageous rebels against strict conformity, but now made into martyrs and rendered more powerful and dangerous in the process.

In their martyrdom they would have had much in common with the first apostles of Jesus, honest workaday fishermen and rough artisans, lit up by a profound cause well worth fighting for and imbued by a genuine love of God. For in the fervent early years of their ministry, the disciples too faced persecution, resolute in shared courage and fortified by the overflowing gifts of the Holy Spirit while upheld by prayerful remembrance of their risen Lord.

It must have seemed to them then that they were indeed on the brink of a transformed world order when all things would be made new and redeemed by love, even as Christ had foretold. In such an inspired mood they surely felt they could do no wrong, because they were guided from on high – and in the beginning this was doubtless true.

At first, wrote Martin, it certainly seemed as if these dedicated followers of Jesus in their attitude of deep devotion *lived the risen life with Christ in heaven; they shared and they possessed with a common will; they kept nothing back so that no one had a store of private means that was unavailable to the fellowship. They were so open to God in prayer and to each other in love... that the Holy Spirit not only infused them with new life but also poured out from them in tumultuous healing power. The gifts of the Holy Spirit... were no mere emotional outpouring of emotional fervour; they were fully-realised phenomena of God's grace constantly renewing a gathering community.*

When the power of God *infuses the cleansed person, the remaking of the entire universe becomes not merely possible but finally inevitable.* Such is the transforming power of contemplative prayer that *glorifies all it illuminates,* but unfortunately in the situation of the disciples, this state of bliss did not persist, as the purity of their devotion became contaminated by expectation of worldly gain. It is a familiar story.

That heaven is its own reward, a doctrine known to all the world's mystics of whatever tradition, was beyond the vision of the later disciples, was Martin's terse comment.

As the earliest Christian communities developed into the future churches, which were to assume greater influence in the disintegrating Roman empire, so did political and spiritual power become entwined. This alliance, wrote Martin, has always been the bane of spirituality because the lord of this world – the prince of darkness known to us as the devil – always seeks to corrupt the faithful and have the final word. The later disciples fell from grace because they became less aware of the crucified Christ in the face of the attractions of the busy world around them. This is our own contemporary problem too. How to reconcile these opposing forces – the sacred and the secular – has always been the most pressing riddle of all spiritual life. Only God can accomplish this reconciliation through the healing power of his Spirit moving within and among us.

* * *

The reality of God resides in the present moment – wherever we may happen to be and in the most ordinary of settings. It is never apart from us and, according to this most natural and uncomplicated of viewpoints we do not need to wait for any second coming. Christ is with us now and all who are converted to him in spirit and truth by virtue of that fact are already living the risen life with him in heaven.

This was Martin's steadfast view, but he also loved above all to celebrate the *exalted communion* of the Eucharist during the central act of formal Christian worship when *in company with the angelic hierarchy and all the host of heaven, we praise God and acknowledge his supreme holiness and his sanctification of the entire universe.*

At that very moment, he reminded his readers, the real presence of Christ is available to us as it was to his disciples at the time of the Last Supper when he first shared consecrated bread and wine with them.

He is always there, but only when we are lifted up to the contemplation of heavenly things can we be available to his constant knocking on the door of our soul. In the same way it is promised that whenever two or three have met together in his name, he is there among us. This is no mere consoling promise but a literal statement of fact. Those who are truly gathered in the spirit of Christ enter a dimension of reality that far transcends earthly consciousness with its constant interruptions of fear, irritation and disharmony...

There is no denying the great beauty of such liturgical worship, but even so the doctrinal side of things is less important than authentic spiritual experience.

'It is what you make of it that counts – that is the crux of the matter', Martin used to tell friends attending his retreats. When he addressed his small and attentive audience in this informal way he conveyed a real sense of the kind of exalted fellowship the apostles must have enjoyed with Jesus.

'When you were with him, things were *different*,' stressed Martin at one of the last retreats he offered, which my wife and I attended in a small convent near our home. He spoke in our midst then with great assurance, as if he himself had been amongst the disciples – and went on to muse: 'When you were with Jesus, you never felt drained. Jesus was the *human face of God* and beamed on those in his company with love.'

He then added thoughtfully: 'God is love. We love because he loved us first.'

That love is their deepest requirement is something that few people would deny, but cannot always admit. Love is truly the universal balm that would heal every wound – but only if it is allowed to work unimpeded by anxiety and doubt. It is in the supportive atmosphere of a well-directed retreat that trust grows and relaxation from the stress and strain of life can come. It is then that love at last can reach the heart and people can blossom inwardly.

Martin never ceased to be amazed at the inner transformation he could sense in individuals attending his retreats. That was a joy to him and whenever he began a new retreat as its spiritual conductor, he would take his place *relaxed and smiling*; this, he wrote, *was no artificial gesture, but rather an outer indication of the inner joy and expectancy* that lay ahead of him.

These fragments of his spiritual instruction were caught on tape twenty years ago and powerfully evoke the quiet authority of his presence, when played back. His manner is quietly unassuming, while his insights are acute, but it is his devotion to Jesus – the great teacher of humanity, who had captured his heart – that strikes you the most.

And what did Jesus think of himself? Nothing at all – he forgot himself, was Martin's forthright answer to his own rhetorical question. The point is Jesus gave of himself fully with love and mixed freely with the common working people, caring little for detailed words of doctrine. His teaching was clear, simple and very beautiful, but always tailored to the capacity of his audience. That was how he did his work.

It was Martin's way as well, so much so that he hardly seemed to be there when he taught. Unassuming as he was, he stood aside and it seemed as if the wisdom poured through him in all its sparkling purity. Martin never considered these inspired words were his own, but were being given to him by the power of the Holy Spirit.

Appointed as a priest, Martin saw it as his privileged task *to speak the word of healing in the name of Christ* whenever he was called upon to do so. By nature he was a shy man – by his own admission *not given to small talk* – yet he cared deeply for people and sought unselfishly to assist them in their troubles.

Father Martin is no longer alive – most precious then are these tapes from a bygone era, preserved with a technology already outdated. The world has moved on, but the reassuring sound of his quiet voice is a valuable reminder of his incisive wisdom.

He did not consider his life had been a particularly happy one, and in common with most people attending his retreats, he had not been spared misfortune. But there is nothing wrong with that, he would tell his audiences, since it is chiefly through difficulties that we grow in compassionate understanding.

He felt ashamed to complain about anything, considering the advantages that had come his way. When you were with Jesus, Martin said, it did not matter what had happened. Despite the worst of tragedies, you still felt all was well; such was the privilege of sharing Christ's company. No matter what had happened, you saw *something far away in the distance – far beyond what had been the very basis of your life.* By the wounds of Jesus, his followers are healed. By accepting our own wounds, we too can be healed.

Chapter 16

Glad to Be Grateful

In my experience, the way to silence is by a gradual dropping-off of thought by immersing oneself in a transparent sea of gratitude for the privilege of being alive at the present moment, and registering that moment as an event in its own right. In this silence the dross of worldly life is gradually cast off, and a vibrant freshness cleanses the soul of all clinging emotional desire. At last one can see clearly and discern the truth which liberates one from the usual bondage to material concerns.

Martin provides in this passage a clear answer to a vital question he has just asked on behalf of his readers: How does one attain the silence which is the very heart of prayer?

He indicates in his reply how a natural sense of gratitude is all it takes to open the hidden door to freedom – a secret door to the inner life, through which the spirit of prayer can easily enter. It is this simple but profound practice of thanksgiving – being grateful for small mercies so the heart can rejoice and be glad – that makes deep prayer possible. At long last then we can recognise God as belonging to our own awareness of reality and finally we can properly offer praise to the supreme energy that guides the destiny of the universe – however we may conceive it.

At the beginning of our spiritual quest for truth, God is just a word to us and it remains entirely up to us to describe in our own terms the creative power that brought us into being and sustains us still. But the freedom to explore the inner life and practise spirituality in the manner that suits us best is something that can never be taken for granted.

The liberating fact that Martin Israel was able to speak so freely about truth, preaching spontaneously in church and other public places whenever invited, testifies to the immense privileges people enjoy in an open and democratic society. How precious this freedom to be oneself in a place of real safety is – but how easily lost within the shadows of fear, oppression and conflict. There is no such thing as absolute security and one can become a victim of violence at any time – even when gathered with others of like mind in the sanctified space of a place of worship. Perhaps there in particular nowadays one is no longer safe. As a Jew, whose distant relatives were harshly persecuted and killed by the Nazis in a synagogue, Martin knew this all too well.

* * *

In good times and bad, as the habit of thanksgiving becomes established in the soul, so our own inner strength grows. It is the tentative dawning of a new life of faith, but it will have to be accompanied by a conscious consecration of the will made possible by a new attitude of openness. We will begin to see for ourselves how this mysterious process of inward transformation has a momentum all of its own as it unfolds and acts unbidden in the most unexpected of ways. Our life is no longer entirely our own, but we are glad to be grateful for we know not what. This is a joy too precious to name and a gift we dare not seize for fear of loss.

What beckons now is a new phase of firm allegiance to the universal values expressed by Jesus during his ministry. The decision to heed this summons to deeper commitment in the service of truth may be slow and silent in coming, but when it does so it is categorical and in the affirmative; it hardly seems our own doing in fact – that is the marvel.

As the living Christ establishes himself more completely in the soul,
so does a measure of self-confidence show itself that is of another

order to the self-inflation that worldly powers confer. While our self-awareness is limited to money, social position (or the lack of it), intellectual brilliance or artistic gifts, it will continue to be in a state of flux. It will balance uneasily in the world of changing values, of vogue attachments that disappear as suddenly as they first arose...

The confirmation of the self, which is the essence of self-confidence, that Christ bestows inculcates a scale of values and indicates a way of life that leads the disciple beyond concern for his prestige to a commitment in love to the whole world. He is no longer interested in his own safety, for he knows dimly yet incontestably that his authentic nature is eternal...

At this point the realisation may have dawned that we have in some measure finally stumbled upon the spiritual freedom that is our birthright; it is likely that one way or another we will have been given a radiant mark or intangible sign that somehow the divine is now acting *within us* in grace unseen. It may make no rational sense and yet we feel different, more open and less resistant to the impacts of life. That much is evident to us.

It is the kind of freedom which with fragrance brings, in Martin's own words, *trust with it so that we can rest with assurance in God's love.* The Lord is recognised at last as not fickle, vengeful or punitive as viewed so often in the Old Testament, but all-merciful – and this loving mercy infuses our very being *changing us into new people.*

In this spiritual freedom, wrote Martin, we need no longer fear psychic contamination nor, on the other hand, do we any longer seek after esoteric knowledge to substantiate our frail self-regard. We are no longer subject to the claims of opposing systems of thought either, for they cannot blur our inner vision of the one God, who transcends all intellectual barriers and racial divisions.

And there is one further indication of a growing detachment

from the allures and illusions of the world. We begin to see for ourselves how neither wealth nor its absence will bring us to the vision of God. In the light of this insight – rich or poor as we may happen to be ourselves – we determine with renewed goodwill to act as best we can in future as a faithful steward of the world's resources while dedicating ourselves to God and His creation in prayer, social action and love; we understand much better too the meaning of those beautiful words from the collect for peace from *The Book of Common Prayer* – 'in whose service is perfect freedom.'

Gone rather thankfully is the questionable liberty to pursue our own ends at all costs; instead we are newly prepared to meet the sorrow of the world in unflinching honesty and with as much compassion as we can muster. It no longer seems altogether too much to ask.

Indeed once we know definitively Christ in the soul as both a principle and personal presence that directs us to an encounter with God, our allegiance to him cannot fail to be total. Martin assures us of this. Now we have been summoned categorically to fulfil the responsibilities that our humanity imposes upon us – as evidenced in the life of Jesus – we may be tempted by the prince of this world as he was, but we will never again be seduced from our high calling; in our own imperfect fashion we will stand firm.

The point is that something within us has changed fundamentally and a deep knot of tension has eased; maybe this has to do with the clarification of a nagging doubt regarding our own true worth. We have found at last forgiveness in our own heart *for our own shortcomings.* By letting go of this chafing resentment towards ourself on account of our perceived failures, a natural sense of our innate dignity has been restored to us through grace; our hesitation has thus been dispelled, bringing the ability to act decisively and with wisdom. This is a gift of the Holy Spirit – and for this perhaps should be reserved the deepest gratitude of all.

Genuine commitment not only renders us more decisive, but brings with it tolerance and moderation in our relationships plus a stable ecumenism of quite a different order to the passive acceptance which borrows ideas indiscriminately to form a somewhat spineless and mixed-up religion with no real roots.

Jesus speaks about the kind of person who hears his words and acts upon them, as someone who *can resist all the threats and hazards of the world, because the foundation of his spiritual edifice is composed of rock – indeed the rock of ages who is God himself.*

Such a person is so secure in his identity, adds Martin that *he can listen with courtesy to all he hears from alien sources;* the free person can inspect all assertions and philosophies with *a warmth of regard that will tend to bring their numerous protagonists into his loving presence where they may experience the living Christ.* This is a place of peace and reconciliation where age-old grievances and enmity on both an individual and global level can begin to find resolution. Once commitment has been *fertilised by the spirit of love, our fear fades as we are able to contain conflicting ideologies no less than rebellious people in our hearts.*

The most inveterate conflicts, wrote Martin, arise from the contents of our own unconscious mind, which in turn are magnified by the dark forces that are so often to be in control of the universe. But once the darkness within us is accepted – even welcomed – the way to reconciliation and healing becomes established. *Christ then reigns in the soul,* transfiguring all that we may encounter in our daily work. In this way the divine presence in the soul leads us patiently onwards towards the future advent of Christ in the world.

The highest point in religious vocation is this work of reconciliation, concluded Martin. Reconciliation is even more holy that ecumenism as love is sown instead of hatred, pardon instead of injury. Just so we too can become instrumental in conveying the peace of God.

Chapter 17

As God Requires

To declare one's allegiance for God does not simply entitle one to dwell in the habitations of the blessed; it places on one the responsibility to get out on God's business into the world of sordid disfigurement, to spread the gospel of peace in places where war alone is known, to be prepared to give up one's life for even the least of our fellow creatures. This life is the soul identity which is to grow in love and wisdom until time itself ends in the coming of glory of Christ in the universe.

Truly to reconcile is wholeheartedly to forgive. We need never forget what has been causing pain and conflict but – consoled by forgiveness graciously offered and received – at least all those concerned can begin anew to find some sort of peace.

In an increasingly troubled world, polarized by deep and intractable conflict, never has there been a greater need for the spirit of reconciliation. Clear recognition of the plain facts concerning this evident truth is invaluable, but it is hardly enough to make much of a difference is it? What is required above all is something more practical. Nothing else but decisive action will do, but we should not consider this for a single moment as a duty remote, a task always to be left to others more qualified than ourselves – those expert negotiators trained in handling disputes of the most tricky and delicate kind. No this particular need is much more pressing, altogether more immediate than that.

It is simpler than we imagine. Actually genuine reconciliation begins with ourselves, exactly where we stand. Only when we have begun to heal our own inner wounds will those in our vicinity begin to benefit from a more beneficent attitude on our part, which no longer seeks confrontation. Only then can a beneficial influence of non violence spread further afield from our example to bring peace and harmony to the world at large.

Still there is a catch. Our goodwill need not go far before it encounters ready opposition, some sort of abrupt hostility to remind us of the abrasive nature of the task before us. Sometimes we *do* have to contend with problematic outer situations, but more often we just seem to be grappling with unfinished business, the messy details of existing circumstances. It is harder than we expected and definitely seems unfair. Is this what conflict resolution is really about?

Perhaps it is in the first instance, but more difficult tests lie ahead – Martin is sure about that and utterly realistic about what real reconciliation entails.

The way of reconciliation soon has to confront the presence of darkness, the force of evil, in the world, and this is where it may appear to be inadequate. To assimilate it unconsciously is as dangerous as ingesting a poisonous substance in one's food. Our goodwill can no more detoxify a poison than neutralize evil, destructive forces in the world – forces which, if given free rein, would lead to a dissolution of all civilized values and bring impenetrable darkness upon the world.

On the other hand, the evil of the world, which finds its reflection in the shadow side of our own personality, cannot be summarily excluded from our gaze, let alone outlawed from our inner life. Reconciliation may tend to underestimate the destructive element in life... but on the other hand, the way of the heart is finally the only direction we know that can lead to universal healing. The wise man fears the spirit of evil, but is not overwhelmed by its threat.

We are always on uncharted territory with any kind of healing work and there are no definite rules or fixed certainties, but our own integrity affords us the best protection and ultimately we have nothing to fear despite the ominous warning Martin gives.

Certain words carry powerful negative associations and nobody feels entirely comfortable hearing about evil, but in the final analysis all created things are under the benevolent domain of God – neither light nor darkness are excluded. Once we have clearly understood this, we will never again become so sorely perplexed by the continual turmoil in the world.

* * *

Strangely dramatic as Martin's description of evil sounds, it is salutary to see how he is not exaggerating its threat, for the dynamics of ignorance by which it is enabled to thrive and the mechanism of suffering, which renders us more prone to its malevolent influence, need to be well understood if they are to be countered and corrected in an effective way.

Falsehood is both insidious and stubborn, while the malice that stems from it may well need to be forcibly constrained before it can be dissolved through right understanding. It sometimes seems as if evil and its minions have actually taken up residence *within us* due to lack of vigilance – and still they lurk in the dark recesses of mind, heart and gut, defying every attempt to reject them.

To what extent do these taunting devils actually exist and how much are they merely fevered figments of disturbed imagination? Only a dawning discernment of what elements are implicated in the struggles of the inner life will begin to inform us that all is contained in our own conscious awareness and not separate from our own reality. Yet adverse influences are real enough on their own level and need to be boldly met and dissolved through deep insight that in essence they have no power over us.

This is wholesome understanding with immense healing potency, because it is based on what is true at the most fundamental level of existence. Here is a compassionate vision of unity that transcends difference and cancels enmity – goodness is the sole reality and evil just a false shadow veiling the sun.

All of this is easy enough to say, but unutterably hard to put into practice. The task of reconciliation is sacred by its very nature, but it also requires us to become a kind of warrior too as we faithfully proceed upon the inner quest for wholeness. It is inherently noble, but in addition it urgently needs to be energised with fresh understanding if it is to be fused with the path of outer service in a way that fully engages the pressing requirements of the world at large, while not being daunted by the numerous obstacles it is bound to encounter.

In a spiritual sense, contagion from adverse influences is much more likely to occur when our natural immunity has been eroded by stress and our defences are down. But it is the way we live our life – what we absorb from the world to nourish us in mind, body and spirit – that has the most bearing on our overall state of health and happiness.

When we turn away from worldliness – howsoever we may conceive it – and look to God or truth instead, we are protected by the love we bear for all things good and the purity of our intention. Such purity naturally returns to the sparkling purity at the source of our being with which it resonates. And when we remain grounded in the deep truth of being, we are completely safe from the assaults of the enemy.

And who is this enemy that assails us? In the first instance it is none other than oneself – for it is our own afflictions of mind and body that disturb our peace and make us suffer; it is in the privacy of our own soul that the ancient battle between good and evil is waged – and God is always on our side.

In spiritual traditions down the ages, analogies drawn from Nature have frequently been utilised to depict the process of cultivating inner virtues resilient enough to withstand the inroads of sorrow and the rigours of the quest for ultimate reality upon which we have embarked.

How deep and invasive are these roots of sorrow, so often watered by bitter resentment that surges up from grinding poverty. In vivid images supporting spiritual instruction to counter suffering, we are instructed how best to till the soil of mind, enriching it with the fertilizing humus of our life experience in order to bring forth an abundant harvest for the good of all. There is so much homely wisdom contained in this advice, and we would do well to heed it.

Not without a dry sense of humour, one ancient Tibetan scripture for example compares the sensible actions of skilled farmers with unskilled ones, who throw away their rubbish and buy manure from other farmers. Those, who are skilled, on the other hand, continue collecting their own rubbish, despite the bad smell and unclean work. When it is ready to be used, they spread it on their land – and out of this they grow their crops. That is a canny way to meet afflictions yet still reap clear advantage from them.

As we continue deliberately to nurture wholesome qualities of mind as the foundation for virtue, more and more of life's natural abundance becomes available to us. It had always been there, but had previously been disregarded – its bounty unnoticed, its great beauty unseen. Now at last our eyes have been opened in a new way, but in the early phase of our newfound faith, this budding sensitivity of the soul is like the emerging growth of a tender, young plant; it needs protection from the chill winds of early spring that swirl around it. From the dense woods beyond the garden in our analogy come other influences of ill fortune that threaten its security. Similarly at the beginning of a dedicated life of prayer involving a definite form of spiritual practice, it is hard not to be deceived by the glittering allure of false promises or disturbed by the menace of what we term evil.

We can do no better than base our spiritual life on the firm foundation of what the Buddhists call 'right thinking'. It is the most auspicious beginning to any endeavour.

In Christian terminology it is then that we commence to climb *the ladder of divine ascent* to mingle with the faithful and join the company of heaven as we invoke the blessings of the communion of saints – those courageous pioneers of spirituality who have gone ahead to make straight the way before us. This, in effect, is what we do also when we associate with people of like mind in fellowship.

As Martin once wrote so graphically, the purpose of shared silence on retreat is *to bring us back into the disturbed world more able to cope with its conflicts, more able to apply the balm of considered reflection to a situation of raw malice.* But we can do none of this through our own good intentions, he emphasised – only God's grace working through us could *achieve the rationally impossible.*

Chapter 18

Dark Face of Reality

Let it be said at once that the genesis of evil is a result of the primary creative act of God, by whom all things are made. God may not have willed the emergence of evil but he could not avoid it when he bestowed free will on his rational creatures, whether human or angelic.

To use that divine gift of free choice on a personal acquisitive basis is much more attractive than offering it in humble dedication to God and one's fellow creatures. The vision of world domination is far more compelling than one of service for the good of the created whole. The end of this fateful choice is seen when we survey the course of selfish action as directed by the evil one, traditionally depicted as a fallen angel of immense resource and malice.

Prior to becoming a priest, Martin Israel was a doctor and pathologist well accustomed to dissection; the incisive outline of the anatomy of evil, which he proceeds to give here bears all the hallmarks of a sure and steady hand. In addition, he was psychically aware and exceptionally skilled in the sober craft of exorcism; it was an unusual blend of qualities to be sure, but a combination that rendered him well qualified to consider such an obscure and troubling subject.

His observations are sombre indeed as he takes pains to place the stark menace of evil in the broadest possible perspective as a relative and not as an absolute truth. But he does so while accepting as fact the grim possibility there is *a conscious, intelligent force of darkness, an overpowering presence of evil in the* universe. And that is a presence of personal identity *no less real in essence than the personal presence of God.*

Any word is just a word and words in themselves have no

actual power until they are charged with the sense of meaning attributed to them. But evil – the most notorious coin in the currency of hatred – has long been allocated a very particular niche of dark significance in human language, indicating as it does the most dire inclination towards the depths of cruelty and heights of moral depravity.

The hard fact of the matter is that evil is not a mistake but the inevitable outcome of ignorance of the true nature of reality; it is the *dark face of reality* to be faced not with fear but viewed in the clear-eyed light of integrity. That is the courageous way of growth into full humanity – and it is the only way in which the affront of evil may be met and properly neutralized.

Good and evil are of course the two dominant, powers that give shape and substance to the world as we know it. They are the fundamental forces of duality within creation, which find their origin in the absolute reality of God that contains them both to all eternity – and which has given them assent to be in the first place.

Positive and negative in their polarity as they will always remain, these opposing qualities of dark and light are inextricably entwined in their dynamic interplay with us too – we belong to the web of life and are not separate from it in any sense. By mysterious chance nevertheless, we have been granted the capacity to stand apart and behold the play of energies that encircle us. We do so in the conscious immediacy of close and careful attention to the moment in hand; it is a matter of awe and wonder, but never a justification for arrogant certainty to be foisted on others. This is the bottom line of our present contemplation on the disturbing anatomy of evil – and the keynote of Martin Israel's profound teachings concerning its profound implications.

In the end the darkness has to inform the light no less than the light to illuminate the darkness. Each has valuable teaching to bestow so that a life beyond the dualities may emerge. This is the life of integrity. It is the life of God beyond the dualities of darkness and light, in which the uncreated light embraces and transfigures both earthly light and subterranean darkness.

A discussion of this sort falls well outside the parameters of conventional debate and is not the sort of thing to go down well with hardened sceptics addicted to proven scientific fact. Such a wary response from mainstream opinion is hardly to be surprised at, but it does a profound subject grave injustice.

This is far more than mere metaphysical speculation. Here Martin is touching upon fundamental disharmony in the universe at the deepest causative level – he is speaking boldly and without reserve of matters visible and invisible, material and subtle; it is a contentious interpretation of rather an unwelcome subject, which is bound to evoke a mood of puzzlement if not outright scorn. Discussions of this kind clearly need to be tempered by a note of reassurance and plenty of realism – only then can we hope to lay the foundations of a mature and responsible spirituality, in which even the most challenging aspects of enquiry are definitely not out of bounds.

Martin would stress that in the normal way of things there is absolutely no need to struggle or stand guard against malevolent forces – our very best protection from all unwelcome influences is our native common sense and the natural healthy functioning of a balanced mind. Evil, as he would often point out, is actually an imbalance – an aberration or departure from what is real. Ultimately there is only the Good and all is well. That is the highest truth, but if ever in doubt about this, he would ask his readers to remember the following:

Avoid duplicity at all times and at any cost, since it opens the door to negativity and gives rise to all manner of complications. Be firm with falsehood – sly offspring of the most forbidding family of ill repute – and never be tempted to collude with it for it will run rings around you and soon entangle you in its web of deceit. Instead stand straight, step back and simply witness its subterfuge. It will never vanquish you then.

There is no need to shrink back before the powers of darkness, because they find their true origin in light; if ever you feel adversely affected by baleful influences, above all never seek to cast them out, but instead *include them in your love* – as that is what they truly long for and therein also lies your greatest safety. This is actually the essence of the ministry of deliverance, in which aberrant elements of unredeemed evil are committed for safe-keeping into the merciful hands of God.

When to the best of your own ability you have done all you can to cope with any sombre concerns you may have, leave well alone and rest in stillness. Deliverance from fear or anxiety may not always come in the shape or manner you quite expect, but once requested in all sincerity it is unfailing in its arrival.

* * *

See how sometimes this fevered thinking just falls away and all you are left with is a deep silence in which nothing at all is truly known. Sometimes indeed simplicity speaks louder than words and any speculation then seems futile. That without doubt is the best place to begin; it is a place where thought is burnt away in stillness – and stillness in turn draws you deeply into the realm of being.

The source of being is the primary reality where Truth abides in fullness; it is the first and last refuge of security where for all intents and purposes evil does not yet exist. There we are truly at home, for as the mind merges softly in the depths of being, so the inescapable sense of duality that belongs to the outer world subsides for a while. At last there is peace.

But peace is not a static state; it endures, but only in a dynamic flow that can never be grasped by the mind. As soon as the focus of our attention returns to outer things, the abrasive nature of external impressions is bound to interrupt our reverie. We seem to live in two distinct spaces then as we strive to straddle a divide that not only defies our best intentions, but also defines the world of opposites.

Here is the root of the stubborn, existential problem that has always baffled mankind; this is the ominous gap of misapprehension that the primal energy of evil ever seeks to exploit. For inner and outer perception may seem to be two separate aspects of reality, but actually they form one total movement within the endless cycles of growth and disintegration.

Life is undivided – naturally existing in oneness; the conviction that we are separate from everything else is the primary delusion responsible for much unnecessary strife and suffering. Original sin is nothing else but a divided consciousness – the false belief that we are separate from God when in truth we are not.

The notion of evil may seem to belong to a vanished age of primitive superstition, and as such may appear altogether irrelevant or out of place in our brash and confident contemporary world. Yet the eternal principles supporting the harmonious functioning of the universe are immutable and cannot be evaded. Evil is implacable and tenacious, but at root it is simply another word for sheer ignorance of natural law. Nevertheless the results of disregarding this law or attempting to selfishly interfere in the harmonious order of the universe are devastating in the extreme – and the day of reckoning will always come in due season.

Many people nowadays find themselves living in high-tech modern societies, which on the surface at any rate appear to have attained a considerable degree of sophistication. Deeper down, however, nothing much has changed and human beings remain as vulnerable to adverse influences as they ever were – prone to deception and all too easily corrupted by false promises.

It is still possible for people to 'sell their soul to the devil'.

When this happens, they effectively become agents of evil and an unconscious channel for abomination. They are capable then of acts of unspeakable barbarity, far beyond their normal capacity for selfish action; ordinary individuals in this way become transformed into monsters, able and willing to perpetrate hideous deeds of cruelty.

In his own life, which had spanned the greater part of the tumultuous twentieth century, Martin Israel had witnessed this terrible sequence of events, as Europe laboured under the savage onslaught of Nazi oppression, seen most graphically of all in the dire scenes of the holocaust. His profound insights regarding the terrible menace of evil remain just as relevant these days as innocent people suffer anew – this time under the scourge of fundamentalist religious ideology, by which all who do not share the narrow interpretation of its adherents' bigoted doctrine are subjected to harsh persecution.

It certainly remained true, Martin wrote, that on one level of reality the soul is immortal, inasmuch as it is God's creation and *God loves every created thing*. But the power of evil, he added *can so dominate a person that his soul consciousness is totally obliterated; he discards his human identity and behaves irrationally like a coarse animal in a large herd, entirely under the direction of the evil one.*

The mob violence, which then occurs is terrifying to envisage and must be even more shocking to behold.

The precious power of discrimination, the fruit of our individual integrity and the very spark of our identity, is blurred and occluded. Devoid of this light of responsibility, the individual is tumultuously overridden by the emotional surge of the crowd and is rendered capable of committing the grossest acts of destructive cruelty, acts that the same person in a state of calm and prayerful awareness would reject in abhorrence.

As an experienced exorcist, Martin Israel had no illusions about the cunning wiles of the devil, whose nature is that of the Antichrist when he gains ascendency over his deluded victims. Giving a chilling account of the evil one's preferred mode of action, Martin described how first of all the awareness of a person is *dulled and duped into a torpid complacency* as his confidence is gained by acts of apparent generosity; the freedom of the will is then *unobtrusively abdicated* so that the victim leans ever more in dependence and trust on the source that has come to his assistance; the evil one *battens on the soul consciousness of his victim whence issues the free will with its capacity to choose and make decisions.* In this way the unguarded awareness lets in malevolent destructive powers that rob the person of his freedom.

The powers of darkness, concluded Martin, have *the capacity to assume a bright glitter that can deceive the unwary if not the very elect.* How then, he asks can we distinguish between the powers of light and darkness in our present climactic world situation? It is climacteric on account of the enormous scientific and technical advancements escalating year by year combined with a general lack of reverence on the part of the majority for the unseen dimension of reality.

We can easily distinguish a power of darkness *by the hatred it exudes* as it works towards the destruction that stands in its path to dominion. By contrast *love emanates from a power of light.* Love acts by giving up itself – even to death if need be – for the sake of its friend, who in the final analysis is everyone around us.

This in turn necessitates a love of oneself so complete, wrote Martin, that one no longer feels threatened by anyone else – let alone has any desire to *abuse, denigrate or destroy him.*

In the mighty conflict of spiritual values, he added soberly, our real adversaries dwell in the intermediary psychic realm. Martin always remained convinced that it was there in the dark and subtle dimensions beyond this world of mortality that the origin of evil is actually to be located – even if it mainly enters the world through the agency of human beings; it is evident that the element we call evil *finds an easy entry in the hearts (or souls) of all those who are unwary, sluggish in the life of prayer and whose private lives are thoughtless and selfish.*

Even a life devoted to social service and praiseworthy political action, Martin insisted, would soon become infiltrated with the forces of evil, if it was not guarded by constant awareness and a primary dedication to God.

Chapter 19

A Measure of Faith

Hatred once fomented, seeks its resolution in such fury that finally no one is left to tell the tale except the Antichrist, the chosen vehicle of the devil, that gloats over the carnage that impassioned men have occasioned – and all in the name of justice.

Power in the hands of those possessed of fanatical zeal soon grips them in a bond of satanic strength as more and more of the tradition of the past is shattered and its treasures fed to the flames...

How could anyone be so scornful of honoured tradition and heedless of ancient beauty? That image of wanton destruction caught on film – the ugly sight of precious artefacts from ancient civilizations being smashed in cruel abandon – stayed with me a very long time as I mused over the pitiless fury of those alienated human beings, lashing out at monuments from days long gone. And they were doing so by giving vent to their hatred of other cultures, just to protect their own strict code of religious observance in a ferocious display of intolerance, the like of which I was horrified to see.

And now there is an associated image – even more distressing – that will not let me be. In my mind's eye I see the black-robed figure of a Muslim woman – apparently taken in adultery – being stoned to death by her accusers, who include her own father. I am filled with sadness at her fate and wonder if there is any limit at all to human brutality.

* * *

How tempting it is to sit in judgement about things we find

repugnant or cannot comprehend, but ultimately there is no truly constructive purpose to be served in pointing the finger of blame at anyone. After all it is well known that hatred always begets further hatred so to prolong suffering. And this only goes to prove yet again that profound love alone has the power to transform bitter emnity at its source to restore the natural balance of harmony.

In view of the tragic sequence of such events in the Middle East in recent times, how strangely prescient seems the statement by Martin Israel which opens this chapter. He was writing about the Reign of Terror initiated by the fanatical Robespierre at the height of the French Revolution at the end of the eighteenth century in which numerous heads rolled beneath the guillotine, but he could well have been referring to the appalling brutality so evident in our own day, which has resisted all attempts to contain and disarm its threat. The essential point is surely this:

Any regime that rules by hatred bears within itself the seeds of its own destruction as eventually the people it holds in subjection rise up and wreak terrible revenge upon their captors. Eventually Robespierre himself, who had wielded supreme power after the execution of French King, Louis XVI, was overthrown in his turn and sent to the guillotine.

Often drawn in his prolific writings to survey the grim and futile cycles of violence that have scarred the collective psyche and perpetuated mankind's suffering down the ages, Martin understandably returned most often to consider the appalling atrocities, which his own generation had witnessed under the scourge of the Nazis during the Second World War.

Regarding Hitler for instance, he noted how it is a fearful thing to see a person consumed with hatred *so that the pleasures of the present hour pass unnoticed behind the film of venom that infiltrates every thought and action.*

The present moment – our point of immediate contact with reality – is *blurred by the emotional turbidity of the psychic atmos-*

phere as this kind of person is *enveloped in a fog of malice that works to separate his soul* from the life-giving power of the Holy Spirit. Such an unredeemed individual lives in a private world *whose form is a battlefield.* At any instant the most innocent bystander may be the target for a terrible outburst of abuse.

The one who is possessed with hatred, wrote Martin, is beyond reason and prayer itself may make no impact on him. One suspected Hitler fell into this category in respect of his blind, irrational hatred of the Jews. How easy it was for the powers of darkness to use such a disturbed human being *for their own nefarious ends of chaos and extinction.*

All hatred is of the devil, no matter how justified it may appear to be since it always ends in the destruction of both the hater and the person who is hated. A sober reading of history will always bear this out, while the only thing that is certain in the fog of war is that once a reign of violence is established it will inevitably escalate.

The human agent or group that initiates the violence *soon becomes the prisoner of demonic forces far outside any rational control.* These dark energies harness the human desire for revenge as well as unutterable delight in destruction for *it is so much easier and more satisfying to cast down than to raise up.*

Martin ends these sombre reflections with a particularly vivid analogy. Once the lid is off the emotional furnace, the steam scalds anyone in the vicinity and *the forces outside make common issue with the pandemonium inside the psyche.* Hell is indeed let loose and its end is total destruction with a return to the primal chaos from which the universe emerged by divine decree.

* * *

To find ourselves outraged by injustice and agonising over the extremes of human cruelty – let alone also troubled by profound existential questions about the dark origins of evil – is often distinctly uncomfortable, but at least it is a definite indication of basic human sanity; much to our credit it is a clear and present sign of a sincere wish to grapple with the deep mysteries of life and death.

We can further rest assured that Martin Israel for one would have thoroughly approved of our incessant quest for meaning, since he regarded doubt as a main doorway to reality and nothing to be ashamed of.

Doubt is a maturing process, he once admitted in an entire book he devoted to the subject – for *in its cold embrace we have left comfort far behind us;* this unwelcome absence of comfort, however, is the very reason we still need to make friends with doubt and make it our own.

Doubt may be *cold, ruthless and a hard task-master,* but it also has its rewards for it sets us on the path that leads to truth.

Certainty cannot tolerate the cold breath of doubt, because in its presence all that is false and tainted shrinks in dismay... Therefore it can be said that doubt illuminates certainty and strengthens it to withstand the forces of destruction that threaten it day by day.

The central insight of mystical understanding is that the great harmony governing the universe *can never be disrupted by human action – even at its most destructive.* There is in other words a *higher order that controls the world's chaos,* but we ourselves are so concerned with our own troubles and ambitions that we mostly remain oblivious of that important fact, the awareness of which could be life-changing for us.

The realisation that in the midst of disorder nevertheless, God knows what he is about and that his love in due course will fill the world with caring, makes all the difference to the quality of our own life; this is what provides an essential key to the meaning of our existence and shows a sure way to the eternity in which we already have our being.

There is one more significant insight that soon comes to a mystically aware person and it is this one:

It is the darkness rather than the light that *is the most fertile medium of growth*. At last we do not need to shun difficulty but can begin to embrace it so that it actually becomes a source of strength instead of a painful reminder of weakness.

What a strange paradox – that doubt should now form the ground of an unshakeable faith in the wholeness of Life as well as providing the basis of beseeching as we continue to pray for harmony to be revealed in the face of the unimaginable calamities that continue to befall the world.

As far as we are concerned, only one thing is certain. As little influence as we may have at any particular moment, we are always required to carry out what lies within our power – for not to do so would be an abrogation of responsibility and a reason for later regret.

In fact the task before us personally is simple and straight-forward. As an individual, it is to stand firm in our own certainty and allow reality to show forth its true face; since this is the way we may best bear witness to truth and in due reverence share solidarity with all created life. And this is how we can contribute the much needed quality of equanimity to ease the anguish of the world, not necessarily knowing exactly how it will come to pass of course; but trusting that it will be so. That is the true measure of a resilient faith.

Chapter 20

The Pain That Heals

In the silence of dark foreboding punctuated by flashes of terror, a remarkable opening of the personality is apt to occur; the soul is laid bare and God is enabled to speak through the spirit... At this point we make the amazing though obvious discovery that the only quality we possess is our own being, and we learn that to let it shine with integrity is the great work of our life.

In this strangely insecure world, as beautiful as ever but rendered fraught by anxiety and vulnerable to savage assault from unknown quarters, agonising moments of dire emergency can erupt without warning into the existence of ordinary, good people going about their normal lives. The devastating result is often untold suffering on a massive scale – pain impossible to articulate and incredibly hard to heal.

Every time news comes through of yet another terrorist outrage or frenzied attack by an isolated loner intent on revenge for some imagined slight, we witness a further example of hell on earth – and may be pushed a step closer to despairing cynicism.

But believe it or not, in the midst of all this anguish, heaven is never far away, and that is what Martin Israel is indicating when he writes of the hidden, creative opportunity afforded by catastrophe as the *soul is laid bare* by indescribable pain.

Heaven can paradoxically *as easily show itself in situations of extreme suffering and danger as in times of prosperity and comfort.* And the reason for this, Martin asserted, is plain enough. When such suffering is *communally borne, and the hazards encompassing everyone make the duration of any individual life an open question, the personal barriers tend to drop and people at last become open with one another. They have little more to lose except their lives, and these are best preserved in an atmosphere of mutual trust.*

This was clearly evident after the unprecedented attack on the New York Trade Center in 2001 and following the London suicide bombings less than four years later – both terrible occasions when great heroism was shown by both victims and rescuers amidst scenes of utter carnage. It remains just as true nowadays as open, democratic societies have again become soft targets in a cruel war, marked out by savage episodes of indiscriminate rampage, spilling horror upon the undefended streets of large cities like Madrid, Mumbai, Nairobi and more recently in the squares and along the boulevards of Paris.

With its sheer brutality and tense aftermath, that particular outrage in November, 2015 was immediately regarded with utmost concern as holding enormous implications for a darker future, signalling a steeply rising global threat from terrorism.

Following all such inconceivably shocking events, the utter devastation and despair consequent upon savage, multiple attacks like these – unprovoked, brazen and merciless as they all were – must have been incredibly distressing to witness.

A grim pattern of violence has thus become established, almost as familiar as it is awful. Brutal assaults without warning on innocent civilians by suicide bombers or heavily armed, militant gunmen, have become a nightmarish reality – a shocking risk of everyday urban living.

* * *

Despite the unmitigated pain inflicted on ordinary people by cowardly assaults upon their basic civil right to freedom, a person's intrinsic worth and natural quality of kindness can never be dismissed or obliterated.

When great suffering is courageously borne, the innate nobility of human beings shines forth, and if a community under threat can band together in solidarity, its quietly shared dignity is beautiful to behold.

Integrity is paramount. Evil seeks to divide, conquer and rule, but recent history has shown that no amount of evil intent can prevail in the face of simple goodness as those vibrant, cosmopolitan cities – rich in ethnic diversity and broadly welcoming to visitors – have stood firm and entire under undeserved attack; fully to realise this same affirmative truth as an individual *is the great work of our life.*

No book comes out of the blue; it is the creative outcome of numerous influences and forged in the sometimes scalding crucible of the author's subjective experience as he fashions his narrative and struggles to find adequate words to convey his intention. Artistic expression is both a reflection of outer events and the inner world made tangible.

So it is that this endeavour too finds its particular but disturbing backdrop against a society grappling with the forbidding challenge posed by an altogether more sinister story than any of the main themes of this book which is concerned above all with deep understanding, mercy and love.

This very different and devious narrative, fashioned by turbulent events in the wider world, relates to the hearts and minds of impressionable, young people being subverted by the perverse reasoning of fundamentalist religious ideology – and urged to commit atrocities in God's name; it is a struggle against what has been termed 'altruistic evil' and is set perhaps to last a generation.

It is a clear indication of Martin Israel's own integrity that, even as the devoted mother, who felt obliged to resign her post as an Anglican priest due to loss of faith following the cruel murder of her beloved daughter in the London tube bombings of 2005, he too steadfastly rejected the easy language of conventional religion that totally fails to measure up to the stark demands of life when times get tough.

With his innate sensitivity bolstered by considerable experience as doctor and clergyman, Martin was never glib in the wise advice he offered and this was what made his own contribution as counsellor and priest so telling and reliable.

As you continue to study his abundant writings in depth, his unflinching honesty in the face of the most challenging questions becomes increasingly apparent. He never sought to turn aside from a person's encounter with anguish but endeavoured to meet and absorb the impact of their suffering with the empathy and compassion that his own pain had already awakened within him.

Martin's keen insights concerning the healing power of pain are central to his unique spiritual approach – they comprise the main thrust of his uplifting message, which in his own words *asserts the creative potential of suffering and looks for a wider ministry of healing than that designed merely to smooth out life's difficulties.*

He fully realised that his essential message would give cold comfort to those wanting instant relief, but for anyone prepared to proceed with their difficulties with tenacious courage, he hoped it would show the way of tried and proven advance *by at least one traveller on the way.* This solitary wayfarer was surely none other than himself, for in responding to the suffering of the many to whom he had witnessed, he knew that his own experience had probably been the starkest of all.

It had become obvious to him that the problem of evil in the face of a living God was not to be solved at a purely intellectual level, since the human mind in grappling with this enigma *brings God down to its own level thereby degrading Him and obscuring its own sight.* On the contrary it was *by traversing the valley where death casts its long shadow* that the sufferer would learn basic truths about his or her own condition.

If one could only find the courage and faith to proceed along the perilous path of self-discovery, one would emerge *a changed person who knows God rather than merely believes in Him.* And the blessed state of equanimity was the precious fruit of such suffering – it was *a winnowing fire* that brings knowledge of the immortal principle that lies at the very root of a person's being.

Yet as always words fall short – they simply cannot convey the full import of *desolation and its aftermath.* We experience desolation *when the very bottom of our private world is removed from us.* Our foundations then have crumbled away from beneath us without warning and in their place is left *a terrifying void,* which can be filled neither by our own efforts or by the well-meaning concern of friends.

When we lose something irreplaceable, wrote Martin, *we enter the well-recorded experience of bereavement.* The most harrowing anguish accompanies the death of a loved one, made even more unendurable when you have lost a beloved child or close relative to inexplicable, savage crime or the futile horrors of war. But in the final analysis, the desolation of loss can follow the disappointment of our dearest hopes in any sphere of endeavour. *The removal of hope is the heart of desolation.*

The personality of man, Martin would go on to explain, *intermingles with all the psychic darkness that has accumulated from the misdeeds and vile thoughts of his forebears since the very dawn of his creation.* But all is not lost since everyone also *has direct access to the ineffable Godhead through the vast communion of loved ones and their emergent energies in the realms beyond human exploration... The little ones of God live courageously a day at a time, knowing intuitively that they are provided for moment by moment even when the future appears hopeless and the present is scarcely bearable.*

It was quite true, Martin admitted, that when inner, psychic darkness descended, even this innate confidence in the providence of God may be obliterated and then someone may have the awful experience of *drowning in a vast sea of dark, meaningless chaos.*

It was probably this experience that induced the victims of severe depression to end their lives – and who could blame them for resorting to this extreme action? Yet if they were able *to* withstand the temptation to quit this life, and instead persist in the name of God who seems to have hidden Himself completely from them, they would quite literally be saved.

The greatest privilege, Martin wrote, that lies in store for the person who has emerged from the valley of the shadow of death is the ability to guide his brethren through that same valley to the delectable mountains that lie beyond it.

Suffering has an electrifying, concentrating effect on the mind. Uneasily one begins to understand that all we possess on a purely personal level needs to be stripped from us before we can know that deeper inner authority that lives in a world beyond the changes of our mortal life. This is the first great lesson of pain.

Yet all our possessions – including of course sound health of body and mind, as well as cherished relationships – need not be discarded for they are not illusions but gifts that God has bestowed upon us to be transformed by our appreciation and love into objects of eternal beauty. As we change, observed Martin, all that appertains to us is changed also and is brought back to God transfigured and resurrected.

From the starkest perspective, however, it is evident that our lives all founder on the rocks of ruin no matter how noteworthy they may have been in terms of what the world calls success. That ruin encompasses three final facts of life: ageing, disease and death. The most important question is this – have we built an inner spiritual body around the eternal soul centre, or has our edifice been fashioned of worldly things that collapse at the full thrust of misfortune?

Martin was convinced that what appears to be a misfortune in the previously evenly tempered life of a successful person is in all probability the thrust of the soul itself, bringing the person, despite himself, to a fuller realisation of God.

On this journey to Truth, we begin to find a sense of inner peace, but real peace, he reminded his readers, is not a state of perpetual immobility or inertia in which nothing more need ever *happen.* It is on the contrary a relationship of intimate communion with God, manifesting itself outwardly in harmonious activity in whatever situation a person finds himself or herself.

Peace is the strength that is given to the weak who have accepted their present impotence and are not ashamed to give themselves in their apparent uselessness to God... Then he offered the following prayer:

Help me, O Lord, to cease from comparing my lot with other people, but rather to see each circumstance, however adverse, as my opportunity for growing into authentic spiritual knowledge. May I thereby be a constant source of inspiration to those around me. One true witness of sanctity is worth all the world's scriptures inasmuch as that person embodies the truth of all written testimonies.

Chapter 21

Agents of Love

We have to come to terms with our own involvement in and respon-
sibility for the disorder that appears to dominate the world. Every
selfish action, every unkind word, every destructive thought has its
repercussions not only on those around us but also in the wider
psychic environment in which we live as spiritual beings. And what
is disordered psychically will make its impact felt in the material
world...

Martin Israel was convinced that our own thoughtless attitudes
play their part in fostering man's inhumanity to man. He also
firmly believed that the psychic disturbance of human beings has
a deep effect on the conditions of the earth, so intimately
connected are human emotions with the physical phenomena of
the natural world.

We tend to blame God for not intervening to arrest the
tragedies of the world, but these are largely of our own creation,
he insisted. And from his unique standpoint as a priest dedicated
to the healing ministry with all that it implied on earth and in the
afterlife too, Martin went much further.

These interminable catastrophes that plague our world are
also doubtless *a product of the demonic powers that reside in the*
psychic realms, and which feed on negative, emotional forces that
emanate from psychologically disturbed human beings...

He asserted that the very future of our planet *depends in no*
small measure on the healing of the psychic atmosphere that envelops it,
because the power of the Holy Spirit has to penetrate this layer before it
can energise the physical world with life.

As the psychic world is cleansed, Martin explained *so will*
ennobling thoughts enter the minds of those who are burdened with the

government of great nations. Then they will be able to grasp their common humanity and the fatherhood of the Almighty, no matter how they envisage Him or what name they give to Him. And then the Spirit of Christ, who gave up His life to save the world, will penetrate their spirit also and renunciation will take the place of the strivings for self-aggrandisement that typify natural man.

At long last demands for victory *will be swallowed up in universal reconciliation and the greatest will be the servant of all.*

This remained Martin's dearest hope as long as he lived. But he never forgot to emphasise that healing prayer and intercession for both the living and the dead *must begin with the person who prays.*

'I cannot be an authentic minister of healing,' he wrote, 'so long as my private life is disordered and my present relationships at home or at my work are unsatisfactory...' 'It is futile for me to pray earnestly for peace in faraway places while there is no peace in me or in my closest relationships. Only when I am at peace in myself will that peace radiate from me to my surroundings and start to heal all those in need.'

'Only then will my prayers on behalf of the world be effective, for an attitude of benevolence and love, such as peace engenders, can have profound psychic effects far away from its original human source. That peace is a fruit of suffering long and gaining an inner wisdom that sees beyond immediate personal gratification.'

It was God's will that all creatures should be healed. Of this Martin had no doubt. But he was equally sure that the healing that God intends is *of a different order* from that envisaged by man, even by most healers who work on a charismatic basis.

We look for outward signs of improvement, *but God sees into the heart.*

We desire relief and a return to normal activity, *but God looks for a transfigured person.*

* * *

Prayer of any real intensity starts with silence before God – for just as in any other deep communication with someone else, we should first of all be quiet and listen properly to them. This silence is contemplative prayer and in the silence, taught Martin, we are at one not only with God as the Holy Spirit but also with the spirit of all those in need. Then *when we remember those people, the power of God passes through our spirit to theirs, for in prayer there is a spiritual bond between all creatures.* So in intercessory prayer we are in effect acting as a bridge, interposing ourselves between God and the person for whom we are praying – and *it is a mystery of God's courtesy to us that he uses us in this great work of healing.*

The essence of all real healing work is to be *an agent of love,* since if the person in travail meets unreserved love, his sufferings are modified and he can come to an appreciation of the meaning of his pain much more rapidly. The love, which a minister of healing like Jesus radiates, is the first experience of divine love the person will have come to know and eventually give to others when he emerges from the gloom of inner darkness into the light of God's creative purpose.

The essence of Martin's radical Christian teaching regarding *the pain that heals* is uncomfortable and sometimes unwelcome, but at least it can easily be summed up and taken to heart:

Only when we have learned the particular lesson that our suffering is here to teach us can *we put away the past pain and enter new fields of endeavour.* In the end it is not so much the pain that is terrible as the apparent meaninglessness that surrounds most suffering like *an impenetrable black pall.*

Only when we can begin to see our own suffering *as a part of universal disorder and can visualise the raising up of the whole world* can we play our proper part *in this liberation from the law of death and disintegration that ends all natural processes.*

As we ourselves proceed to offer up profoundly healing

prayers of intercession – deliberately or spontaneously when moved by compassion to do so – we find ourselves engaging in what is a sacred duty. And as we participate in this vital work, we are beginning to play a part in alleviating the universal suffering that in truth is a necessary part of the growth into full humanity.

Genuine contemplative prayer – not just the recitation of set prayers – is far-reaching indeed and benefits not only the living wherever they may happen to be in this world, but extends into the unknown realms of the afterlife to heal the deceased. This, in accordance with ancient tradition, was Martin's firm conviction – and in a piece of most significant and highly charged writing he went on to make observations, most of which would hardly have found favour in the furthermost corners of either religious or secular opinion.

'The importance of prayers for the dead cannot be over-emphasised, and it is the entities without faith that need our solicitude far more than those who have lived and died in faith,' he wrote.

'If the necessity for intercessory prayer is accepted for the indifferent discarnate entities that populate the intermediate zones close to our earth, how much more important it must be for those really evil people who, in their lives, killed millions of their fellow men and filled the world with hatred and violence.

'In their psychic hell they are in blackness and enveloped in the world's hatred, especially in the loathing of the descendants of their victims and perhaps some of the victims also. The psychic atmosphere of evil is not only appalling in itself; it also casts its noxious influence over the whole cosmos.'

Hell, added Martin, was not a place, *but a psychic atmosphere of dereliction, isolation and purposeless, repetitive motion.* That being so, compassion was most sorely needed – not just condemnation for figures of hate, who were understandably regarded as despicable outcasts.

We should remember in love not only those who have lived good lives while on earth, but also the criminals, the torturers, the persecutors and those who have seduced the world in their time with vain philosophies and noxious ideologies.

Such work of intercession for the most evil men now departed this life is *assuredly a dedicated ministry* and he definitely did not recommend it to *those unschooled in the life of prayer.* The majority drawn to intercession were best employed in remembering people in special, present need, but others whose life was *centred on God, and to whom prayer is as essential for the life of the soul as breathing is for that of the body, should pray ceaselessly for all souls in misery in the outer reaches of the life beyond death.*

Chapter 22

Impossible Questions

God is indeed eternally alive and is closer to his own creation than its own self-awareness. Yet at the same time an enormous distance separates the two; the divine transcendence allows the creature to get on with its own affairs without God interfering like an over-solicitous parent of the old school, never letting its children live their own lives. If God's creation were anything other than perfect, he would be available like an artisan to put the mechanism right, but instead he has arranged a self-perpetuating universe that may hold out for many million years, by which time we may hope that the second coming of Christ may have altered the very scheme of reality.

Martin Israel is always rigorous in analysis, but here he seems faintly quizzical too as if amused at the endless ramifications of what is obviously an unanswerable paradox. Can the earth really be regarded as a perfect abode for human beings when its inhabitants are not only subject to natural disasters like hurricanes, floods and droughts, but also fall prey to all kinds of infections while becoming prone to degenerative diseases and sad infirmity? In any case who would really want to reach an advanced age if the quality of living was to be seriously blighted by dementia, blindness or paralysis?

The wise person, Martin reflected, realises that *it is these very impediments that sets the seal on human greatness,* for when we are diminished beyond previous recognition Christ-like qualities to be deeply honoured are at last enabled to shine forth from us. If indeed we take Christ as our example, we may begin to see what our pattern of life ought to be, yet in striving for perfection according to merely human understanding *we may evade the encounter with a God who is as much master of evil as of goodness, of pain as of pleasure, of darkness as of light.*

The unfathomable mystery of God's all-encompassing goodness in unity with all created things is proclaimed by the fact that he is plainly the ultimate originator of evil and then seems to stand aside to allow its nefarious operations in which the primal forces of disorder and dissolution are given full scope to produce total chaos so returning creation to the formless void from which it emerged.

Certainly this would not have come about if God *had been more careful in the creation of his cosmos.* Yet if the Creator had *not* given *his prize creature* – that is to say the human being – a high degree of intelligence combined with a great power of imagination and a free will, there would have been *a sheep-like subservience to the divine will.* The forbidden fruit would have remained uneaten and we would all be mouldering in paradise – however, then our whole lifespan would have been spent in sleep, for *when there is no challenge, there is no movement, let alone growth.*

If only God had planted that wretched tree bearing the fruit of the knowledge of good and evil elsewhere, he need not have spent any time warning us not to tamper with it. And if he had insisted on planting the tree, he could have at least excluded from its ambience that nasty serpent, the very symbol of all that is evil in his creation, and what we now call the devil. And who created that serpent if not God?

That rather light-hearted diversion, concluded Martin, brings us to the heart of the matter. The presence of what we call evil in the world is not some ghastly mistake. Not at all – *evil is an integral part of creation, as much a reality as what we call good, and we have to learn to live creatively with the whole.* The middle way between the extremes of a stultifying goodness and a destroying evil is a balance that can use all circumstances in life constructively.

Of one thing Martin was convinced: God loves everything he has made and nothing is condemned to total destruction. Human recalcitrance can undoubtedly precipitate intense suffering, but this is only produced by the creature in its foolish conflict with the cosmic law of harmony.

God is often presented in the Old Testament as a wrathful figure standing in judgement and wreaking vengeance upon his erring subjects, but Martin was adamant he could never love a capricious tyrant like that.

He knew God only as love and the love of which he spoke and wrote was *no sentimental outpouring of effusive sympathy that does little to share the burden or relieve the pain.* It was on the contrary *the very power that enables growth to take place even in the midst of terrible suffering.*

And he was not spared a considerable measure of that suffering himself. Martin was a mild man, but as a priest he felt summoned to take on by his own admission the *specialized and dangerous work* of exorcism and the ministry of deliverance. Like St. Paul of Tarsus, the great apostle of Jesus whom he most admired, he saw it as his vocation to explore the intermediate psychic dimensions that fall between earth and heaven.

Supportive rescue work of disembodied entities in the unseen realms through rapt prayer was an extraordinary facet of his healing mission and of course it set him apart from other clergy in no uncertain manner – yet he was never deterred by the prospect of being an outsider.

Taking St. Paul as his pioneering mentor, Martin too was ineluctably drawn to understand the 'principalities and powers' involved in the seemingly endless conflict between good and evil and as ever he recorded his findings with the scrupulous care of someone from a medical background well schooled in scientific method.

Forthright in disapproval but wearily realistic concerning the prejudice prevailing in his day regarding psychic matters, he was well aware of the tendency in our so-called 'enlightened times' to *demythologize the supra-rational aspect of the Bible, to relegate all kinds of inexplicable events to the realms of myth or illusion so that human reason is the measure both of and for all things.*

How convenient it was for the materialist to be able to dismiss all such beliefs in *powers intermediate,* to be able to swiftly repudiate any such *expositions of psychic presence* in order to consign all paranormal experience without further ado into the category of unproven psychology. For according to established scientific opinion, anyone with metaphysical views have deluded minds, since the material world alone is real and anything beyond its reach is pure illusion.

To many people, wrote Martin, the detached agnostic type of scientist is *the ultimate purveyor of truth* and so he ought to be, but unfortunately his mind has its prejudices no less than the minds of naturally religious people; after all he too *is a mere human being subject to our common frailties.*

Martin bemoaned how otherwise sensible humanists and triumphant religious people alike *often share an unpleasantly strident arrogance* that tends to silence all other opinions and appear to have *attained a victory.* But the truth is greater than any human opinion, he stressed; when we follow it *we are led into many strange encounters that would have shocked us in the green period of our youthful assurance.*

The person who is naturally sensitive psychically *is in the possession of a gift that is both serviceable to others and wounding to himself.* It is a capacity that must be *used with reverence and the call is from God not man,* but if the psychic gift is to be of real use to humanity both it and humanity need to be educated. Arcane subjects like the paranormal need to be *delivered from the glamour* that surrounds them, while humanity needs to be properly informed of the serious issues raised by the psychic dimension – *that it is neither mental delusion nor systematized fraud; neither primitive superstition nor the antics of a sophisticated generation;*

neither inevitably evil like black magic nor the casting out of malign spells, nor attempting to determine or influence the future by occult techniques.

Not at all. Psychic sensitivity, observed Martin, is much more commonplace than all this *compendium of nonsense.* Politely reticent in everyday life, yet he could be fiercely outspoken concerning things he deeply cared about – and much preferred to talk from personal experience than *hide behind vague generalizations.*

In his extensive writings he frequently considered this mysterious realm that for him *transcended but never occluded the material basis of everyday existence.* Describing this subtle dimension in terms of colour as *of solemn hue,* he wrote persuasively of the dark aura he perceived around the atmosphere of certain individuals, knowing intuitively even as a child that such people were unwholesome, even as particular places could be too when pervaded with a dark atmosphere. His acute psychic sensitivity in early life made him aware of ' presences' sensed in a mood of gloom whose origin he could not define. Some were probably the restless spirits of the dead, he later believed, while a few had a darker more forbidding emanation. These filled him with terror but by *holding fast to God* he felt supported and guided in this *uncharted terrain of dark radiance.*

Those early psychic experiences were to play an important part in Martin's later work in the ministry of healing and deliverance. Priestly orders were to confer on him a spiritual authority that he lacked as a layman, even though he had been deeply involved in conducting retreats, counselling and healing before he became ordained.

Unusually skilled in straddling the material and intangible, unseen worlds, he would in due course be made Church of England exorcist for the diocese of London no less. It was an extraordinary appointment to be sure and it carried grave responsibilities, but first he would need to be initiated into the hazardous nature of this strange but valuable work that he regarded as having been *thrust upon him* – but which he would never shirk. During an interview at the very beginning of his parish work, he encountered a situation of the most disturbing kind that would become the prototype of many unusual counselling sessions in the course of his profound, pastoral duties.

* * *

The visitor arriving for consultation on this occasion early on in his ministry was in a state of near-suicidal darkness. He was a man of artistic temperament but employed in the financial world, and he explained how had been suffering from repeated bouts of severe depression, which his doctors were unable to cure with drugs.

Martin immediately became aware of a malign presence overshadowing this person and asked whether anyone close to him had recently died. The visitor replied that a colleague in a position of authority over him had just lost his life in circumstances that suggested suicide. What was so strange was the fact that the deceased man had always behaved tyrannically towards him, making his life at work a constant misery. One might have expected such a death to come almost as a relief, but instead the depression of the visitor had intensified.

It came to Martin *as a thundering shock* that the dead man was obsessing the psyche of his sensitive colleague with the intention of driving him also to suicide – and the evil of this situation was overwhelming.

Without further ado Martin bade the 'spirit' of the deceased one to *depart forthwith into the protective custody of God* – and at once the suicidal depression lifted from the sensitive visitor. Remarkably his mind recovered normal emotional balance at once and he was able to leave the church in a state of calm relief.

The depression, Martin admitted, did occasionally recur, but there was never again so terrible an episode that suicide was threatened.

It was evident to the newly appointed priest that his visitor was naturally sensitive psychically speaking and needed to be instructed how to control the psychic faculty. Once that had been accomplished, the person was in control of his life – and perhaps it was not surprising that he subsequently left the world of finance for that of art. It was a memorable beginning to Martin's healing mission, but the dramatic experience served as a salutary reminder for him of what powerful, dark forces were involved in the ministry of deliverance; it also made abundantly clear for him how such hazardous, inner work could only be effectively accomplished under God's protection and according to divine dispensation.

Chapter 23

Dark Victory

I thank you, O Lord, for the constant abrasiveness of life's encounters, which bring me closer to my true nature unadorned by fantasies and illusions.

Here is a prayer, succinct and curiously spare in terms of style – for sheer immediacy unforgettable by virtue of its straightforward candour. It certainly seems to encapsulate exactly the strident and stressful tone so characteristic of contemporary living.

Composed especially by Martin along with other meditations for due reflection by his readers, the very particular choice of words is richly expressive of his own essential humanity, which he never sought to conceal from himself and encouraged in others.

A saintly man he may well have been, but a sanctimonious portrait that did not take full account of his foibles would have been anathema to him. Martin was an acutely shy and sensitive person, who could scarcely survive and prosper without adequate time and space for solitary reflection. He stands out for his rare qualities of wisdom and equanimity, but he never lost an opportunity to admit that he was plagued by 'the black dog' of insistent depression and was prone to irascibility from overwork.

His uniquely thoughtful personality encompassed a curious combination of qualities both sober and daring, other-worldly and down-to-earth. He would refer routinely to the angelic realms in the afterlife – delineating in splendid detail its elaborate hierarchy from the overarching heights of heaven down to its abysmal and demonic depths where dark angels dwell – but was governed all the while by scrupulous, scientific caution in this world that left no stone unturned in examining the furthest and deepest implications of an authentic spirituality simply designed to help people cope more harmoniously and happily in daily life.

When he was brusque with troublesome people on the telephone for instance, his guardian angel in whom he believed *absolutely*, helped him keep his temper cool so he *was not in danger of exploding.* He knew this hardly sounded spiritual, but if one was confronted *by a veritable mountain of work*, such irritability might become slightly more understandable – and to understand all is to become increasingly tolerant; the end of *all this naked display of impatience is to attain that very understanding.*

'Though I am not a particularly guilt-ridden person,' he wrote, 'when one is traversing the spiritual path even small irregularities may cause one to stumble. This is the price one pays for spiritual progress. What might cause the "man in the street" to shrug his shoulders in complete unconcern is of discomfort to a person of spiritual awareness.'

* * *

Martin frankly acknowledged his human failings and utilised any conceivable opportunities they offered for growth into wisdom, but he never fully *identified* with the inevitable limitations of personality. In this sense he drew a clear distinction between his essential self (or soul) and his mind – even as he did between the mind and physical brain. He regarded this distinction between consciousness and physicality as crucial – absolutely pivotal regarding the vital difference between materialistic and existential spiritual philosophy, which in his wide-ranging approach included the subtle, psychic dimensions of reality, so often discountenanced by scientific and secular opinion.

In the eyes of the mystic, disputes between sacred and secular are fallacious, because reality exists in oneness, but on a relative level where distinctions hold good the *problem is perennial: Is the mind a product of the brain or has it an independent existence, working through the medium of the brain while we are still alive, but capable of a continuing existence once the body dies?*

The weight of scientific opinion is strongly weighted in favour of the first conclusion – that mind and brain are inseparable and that *when you are dead, you certainly are dead.* Nevertheless people of spiritual persuasion the world over are less sure, Martin pointed out, since *all the major religions envisage some sort of posthumous survival of the personality without the body to direct it.*

The data of psychical research (or parapsychology) seemed to suggest that mind can act independently of the brain both during life and after death – Martin acknowledged that – but the problem lay in the *unpredictability* of the phenomena and the seeming impossibility of reproducing them at will.

The scientific view insists, *quite reasonably* he believed, on the *reproducibility of its data,* but it was evident that the mind-body problem could not be solved scientifically. Fortunately there are other modalities of truth besides the scientific model.

For Martin – still very much on this earth – it was of cardinal relevance to ask: *Is depression a disease of the brain or is it a reaction to unfortunate circumstances earlier on in one's life?* From his own searing experience, he had come down *unequivocally in favour of the psychiatric view* that depression is due to cerebral dysfunction, which can usually be alleviated by antidepressant drugs. But if a person was more able to cope with their character problems, perhaps they might not react so negatively that a brain reaction became inevitable. This is where he saw psychotherapy as having such valuable application.

In his reflections upon these lines, Martin in his own day was pioneering a new paradigm regarding the vital importance of the inner life as a causative factor in illness, both physical and mental. He was a firm believer in preventative medicine, and would have doubtless been glad to see how it is increasingly coming into its own in alternative circles at least.

However, he would not have been surprised to note that such conjectures continue to be viewed with hesitant scepticism in most quarters of mainstream society – ever in thrall to scientific pronouncements. Even so, while resistance to more penetrating inquiry about the nature of human consciousness remains strong, there are promising signs of a more open attitude gaining ground, as the frontiers of science continue to be extended. In time perhaps even the most rigid of materialistic assumptions will be demolished.

So things may be better now, but writing in 1995, Martin recalled with discomfort the uneasy response he had elicited from medical colleagues when he had attended some fifteen years earlier a conference on causative factors in cancer. During an animated discussion about external environmental factors relating to that dread disease, he had ventured to suggest *with great trepidation* that professionals such as they were *should also consider the inner life of the patient.*

'The deadly silence that ensued cowed me into a state of near paralysis,' he noted and added:

'I escaped from this group as quickly as possible, my innate shyness reaching a nadir of shame (as if I had been guilty of an indecent act) as I drove home from the provincial centre.'

The person, who had put Martin's name forward as a potential contributor, later seemed to have no recollection of his 'contribution' and merely said that the conference had not been a conspicuous success. Martin, for his part, was rather relieved that his *indiscretion had apparently gone largely unnoticed amongst the learned workers present at the gathering.*

Our inner life, observed Martin, included the state of mind our background has evoked through our past experience with all its influences for good and ill. But there may at least in some people dwell *the intimation of the mystic that lies embedded but largely disregarded in the depths of the psyche* of a surprisingly large number of individuals. This awareness hints that there is more to life than merely what confronts us in the course of bruising, encounters with the external world.

It may not be difficult, he admitted, *to dismiss these transcendent stirrings* as emotional compensation to render present suffering endurable. Yet the fact that they often seem to come out of the blue and *raise the person from a persistent position of complaint to one of patience and endurance with a song of joy in the heart* clearly shows their authenticity.

If someone suffering *the pains of mortality,* whether through outer circumstances or inner torment, *can still present a smiling face to the world* and behave with unselfish, consideration for others, that person must be close to the divine source – however we may choose to define it.

Human folly usually parodies wisdom most pathetically when it solemnly gives dogmatic judgements about matters of which it is blindly ignorant.

The familiar near-death experience, he pointed out, is written off accordingly by nearly all psychologists as *merely a giant hallucination conjured up by a failing brain.* Yet one could hardly dismiss so easily the marked, moral and spiritual uplift this so-called hallucination produced in subsequent daily life.

* * *

Throughout Martin's teachings, the central issue of the inner life and how best it may be fostered looms large – it was the focus of all the counselling he offered. Whatever predisposition to melancholia he personally possessed, it had been complicated by the physical abuse he had endured from his own father and the consequential low, self-esteem, which had made his youth and early adult years a misery. Whatever insights he gleaned from his own suffering, he freely passed on to his readers and students.

Whenever possible he would outline the well-trodden, traditional route to spiritual emancipation, tried and tested down the centuries, which had seen him through his most grievous bouts of depression. It was a simple way to interior freedom from afflictive emotions, by which one learns to stand back as witness, ceasing to identify fully with their turbulence. To allow oneself to experience any emotion to the uttermost, is to go to journey's end. It is like entering a fierce fire that burns away all the dross, leaving only the essentials untouched by the inferno.

Close identification with our most intimate feelings is linked to an even deeper belief that our body-mind is our true self. Such a fundamental conviction – the very basis of our mortal identity – is deeply rooted and is only gradually dissolved through the inner, spiritual work of right understanding.

A crucial turning-point is reached as we begin to recognise the very life-force within us as the indwelling spirit. As this fresh and most liberating conviction dawns, close attachment to attributes of mind and body begin to ease and the unforced sense of intrinsic unity with the whole of existence arises.

It is altogether a new beginning and it will have considerable bearing on our attitude to the remainder of this life. Perhaps it will also deeply affect our view of the life to come, which beckons far beyond the most daunting, final frontier of the grave.

For if the life within us is of the nature of eternity, in essence we too must share in that supreme reality whether we remain embodied or not. It is a matter of faith that this is so, but at least we can live according to that possibility – and see if our own subjective experience bears out our intimations of immortality.

In the meantime we are obliged to witness as long as we live the continual interplay of contrasting moods within the field of awareness according to our state of bodily health and circumstances governing our life and relationships.

When, wrote Martin, *we can get to know the inner manifestations of various patterns of personal emotion, we can use our lives more creatively.* And as we become increasingly capable of losing ourselves in loving service of other people, so we find ourselves able to *transcend the apparently insurmountable barriers of immortality* prior to discovery of *the unitive consciousness of the mystic.*

Nothing could be more excellent, he said, than this realisation that *there is nothing completely valueless in our lives* – for even something as burdensome as depression can then be the means of understanding other people more compassionately.

Every mood has something to offer the sensitive person; all moods are stepping-stones to an awareness of the totality of life and of our place in eternity.

Chapter 24

Day of Reckoning

The acceptance of life's continuation beyond the death of its physical vehicle is crucial to our deeper understanding of suffering and its effect in building the person's soul structure... One thing is apparent: even those who live to a ripe old age and have spiritual understanding know how little they have achieved on the level of inner sanctification at the time of their death. We fail in love day after day, and the higher the degree of our spiritual understanding the more tragically aware are we of our lack of love to those less fortunate than we are. Without survival of death, there could be no growth of the person into something of the measure of a fully grown son of God.

In the Old Testament of the Bible, wrote Martin Israel, there is a strong association between impure conduct and misfortune. How much of our present suffering on a personal or communal level is due to the misdeeds we committed in the past? And if there is a direct link between past sin and present pains, can the past extend into a previous mode of existence before the present life?

In the Hindu and Buddhist traditions, as Martin often pointed out, the concept of 'karma' is very important – cherished as stark reminder of the moral law of cause and effect persisting throughout a succession of lives in their philosophy of reincarnation. We have all lived many times before these ancient spiritual traditions affirm – and we cannot possibly evade responsibility for our actions. This universal law is plainly seen in action in the most minute details of our daily life – let alone in previous lives we may or may not have lived according to speculation that will probably always remain beyond certain proof despite much interesting psychical research.

Personally Martin was not *altogether sorry* that there was not as yet any scientifically acceptable proof of survival, as he did not think we deserve it in our present state of spiritual awareness; in the end he considered it is the intimations that come to a person directly that were most likely to guide him into the *hazy area of psychical knowledge* in which trends in the afterlife may perhaps be discerned.

As a doctor Martin also knew all too clearly how a good deal of our suffering is a direct result of unfortunate actions in the years behind us. The unwise eating habits of those who live in privileged societies for instance bring their own bitter harvest of grim, physical disorders, while the malnutrition of those who inhabit the underdeveloped regions of the world leads to the premature death of large swathes of vulnerable children and adults. Similarly our present permissive attitude to personal morality is not without due retribution in its toll of sexual disease, drug abuse and emotional breakdown.

In just the same way as there is plainly a relationship between states of psychological disturbance and bodily ill-health, so too unassuaged guilt for wrongful actions in the past will eventually demolish the physical and mental health of the sinner until he confesses his past misdeeds to God and seeks absolution.

Many people, however, Martin noted, are so insensitive to the feelings of others and so obtuse morally that they simply do not realise how their selfishness is cutting them off from full communion with others and separating them from the power of the Holy Spirit, who gives us life and brings us to the full fruition of our personality. Yet the moral law is *contravened at our peril*, he points out; for a long time we may seem to escape unnoticed, but in due course the finger of justice points directly at us – and then suffering well and truly begins.

* * *

These incisive reflections are drawn from Martin's fourth book, published some thirty-five years ago, and appropriately entitled *Smouldering Fire* to describe the slow but steady work of the Holy Spirit within the hidden recesses of one's mind and heart. How strikingly prescient his keen observations remain as we witness in our own era the appalling suffering being inflicted upon countless innocent people by opposing sides, united in their cruel determination to prevail at all costs in a brutally protracted conflict that has torn apart the Middle East and spread fear and chaos far and wide.

Depravity on the scale seen in our midst in recent times would certainly seem to represent, according to Martin's sober warning, *the confrontation with naked evil* – the most terrible test of all from which anyone unprepared should rightly flinch.

The very future of the world may depend, he said, *on the manner in which this test is concluded* – for we cannot expect to withstand the impact of concentrated evil in our normal *dimly-aware state of consciousness* without being overwhelmed by it. The stark fact of the matter is that we need God's grace to protect us from the psychic darkness that *emanates from the cosmic spheres and is projected into the personalities of receptive human beings.*

It was clear, was it not, that unspeakably evil things had been done to helpless individuals since the birth of human consciousness and bestial acts have been perpetrated against racial and religious groups that have led to their annihilation?

The manifest triumph of evil over good that occurs in the annals of history... is surely the greatest stumbling-block to the belief in God. To the rational mind there is no God or this God is either impotent or as brutal as the creation.

There was certainly no intellectual answer to the fact of evil, Martin felt. Yet perhaps we may come to realise that evil too has its place in the scheme of things to set us free from *the comfortable world of mediocrity.* For the world we inhabit is a dynamic form that changes constantly, undergoing corruption, death and renewal, as it moves towards its destiny *in unceasing hope of total redemption.*

In the great confrontation between the life that affirms and the life that denies – between the power that lifts everything up to God and the power that erases and reduces things to nothing – between the individual who moves to realisation of the divinity within him and the person who *affirms the bestiality deeply set in the bodily consciousness,* it is definitely decreed *that the lesser must have its time of triumph over the greater. This is the unbearable tragedy of mortal life.*

It seems to me that we cannot help but notice what befalls our troubled world, but have no right to sit in final judgement about it. And this is simply because the causes of international conflict are so complex and deep-rooted. Nevertheless at this deeply disturbing time, any person of goodwill will certainly view with horror the unscrupulous exploitation of youth through radicalisation by ruthless, religious fanatics as they gather vulnerable recruits to their pernicious ideology. The narrative of such cynical extremists is evidently both debased and flawed as they chillingly utilise the noble idea of martyrdom, not only to beguile potential followers, but also as a powerful political tool of coercion to strike terror into the hearts of their enemies through brutal executions and other atrocities beyond the pale of human decency. The day of reckoning will surely come – that much is obvious – it is just a question of how and when the balance of harmony will be restored.

Actually the precise manner in which the situation will be rectified is not even our concern – we only need to remember that the law of cause and effect is absolute and can never be evaded. We may gather great strength and solace from the clear knowledge that nobody can escape the moral consequences of their actions. Retribution will certainly follow just as the 'wheel of the oxcart follows the hoof print of the animal that draws it,' according to ancient Buddhist analogy in *The Dhammapada.*

Retributive suffering is inevitable, but it becomes redemptive as soon as anyone begins to take sober responsibility for their actions.

At that crucial moment, the individual ceases to amass adverse karma as he or she starts to live according to spiritual law instead of by thoughtless selfishness. Although as Martin points out, the pain does not diminish, it is no longer submitted to *with the blind incomprehension of an animal being goaded by a brutal overseer.* The awakened person begins to see the deeper significance of his travail, so that a sense of purpose informs his suffering.

In redemptive suffering the person in travail has *passed beyond outraged complaints and comforting thoughts of future recompense* to a state of acceptance in which he is *one with his meanest brother as well as with the crucified Christ,* who is crucified afresh whenever men behave with cruelty to one another.

There is just one further vital point to make. Genuine martyrdom can never be exploited for selfish ends, stressed Martin. It is forced on a saintly person by circumstances beyond his control and never assumed by an act of personal will. Willed martyrdom *merges imperceptibly into exhibitionism on the one hand and suicide on the other.* If the sacrifice of the self retains undertones of resentment, that sacrifice will lead to such further hatred on its own behalf *that the forces of evil will gain a victory undreamed of by the self-appointed martyr.*

Chapter 25

The Gift of Age

We start to make our old age in our youth; if we were concerned about other people when we were young, that concern will show itself in our faces and general demeanour when we are of advanced years... A person of grace respects the feelings and attitudes of other, showing a courtesy that is the foundation of a sound relationship which may in time mature to a warm friendship... The experience of a well-tested adult life brings with it this grace – and a wise elderly person has something precious to offer.

How very true this is. Grace is an inner blessing, wrote Martin with kindly assurance; it comes from God and we are its servants. *It lubricates the machinery of common life in the form of considerate deeds towards other people,* and if we live in the conscious awareness of the wants of others *grace informs our actions as it civilizes our attitudes.* Even if we were not conspicuously gracious when we were young and healthy, the experience of life will deepen our sympathies as we too partake of some of the heart-break that punctuates mortal life.

The great gift of age is this hard-won experience – experience of people, of circumstances, of personal humiliation, of forgiveness and growth, of the things of this world and of their gradual relinquishment.

Death will follow sooner or later – an entirely natural but crucial stage in the development of all living creatures in which they are obliged to renounce their present mode of life and enter an unknown existence, of whose reality the human intellect can give little assurance and whose continuity is at best *a shadow cast by thoughts of the night.*

Yet a human being *dies day by day if he is living properly.*

As fresh demands are made and new insights are given, so a person dies to the old and is reborn in the new life. But let it not be imagined, stressed Martin, that the forces that encompass these partial deaths during life are pleasant or benign. *They are harsh, invariably bitter and often vicious.* Rivalry, disease, mental breakdown, persecution, bereavement – the collapse of one's hopes due to the betrayal of those whom one regarded as friends – are cruel facts of life. They cannot – indeed must not – be diminished, explained away or dismissed as *illusory products of false thinking.* To do so, he concluded, would be *a betrayal of all that is noble in human nature.*

It would also be a betrayal of the dark side of life, which must be given its weight too. Those who speak figuratively of *giving even the devil his due* are nearer the truth than they are probably aware.

We cannot escape the dark, demonic influences that overshadow life in the world of becoming for they in addition have their part to play. Until they are acknowledged, Martin wrote decisively, *there can be no end to darkness, no completion of the suffering of mortal creatures – no victory of immortality over transience.*

The supreme death that confronts us all while we are still alive in the world is the tragedy of bereavement. When a loved one dies, something deep in us also dies – and a void remains. The one on whom we have greatly depended for emotional sustenance has been taken away and *a chasm of meaninglessness* is all that remains. But if only *this partial breach of the soul* can be healed by the introduction of new, more widely-based relationships in which service and concern for others rather than personal comfort are the chief factors, *we may start to move beyond death to life even in this world.*

What Martin writes here is of the greatest relevance for my own life as I approach the final chapters of this account of his remarkable healing ministry. Only gradually have I come to realise that, from the days I came of age, my experience has been defined to a great extent by the loss of my mother to cancer at the early age of fifty-four, just two years after a devastating head-on car crash in which she and my father were involved.

I was the youngest of her three sons – and born on her birthday, which fell on November 23rd. There was naturally a particularly close bond between us – and I was distraught when the grievous illness she underwent soon after this catastrophic accident transformed her in a matter of months before my eyes from a beautiful woman into a reduced figure, pitiful to behold. The experience of seeing my mother in hospital in the weeks before she died scarred my psyche more than can be adequately described – and left me with a deep fear of cancer, which took years of inner work to process. If this profound fear of mortal illness has by now to a large extent been healed, it is only by the loving grace of God that this is so.

However, in the process, I have been sustained throughout by wholesome spiritual teachings, including those of Martin Israel, which are outlined in this book – and which address above all *the healing power of pain*. There is a world of profound meaning for me in this simple directive to embrace difficulty and suffering instead of shunning the ills that are an intrinsic part of living. Within these age-old spiritual teachings that integrate the darkness and light of experience into the supreme goodness of God is scope for lifelong contemplation.

This then is the secret as communicated by Martin. Death not only marks the inevitable end of physical existence, but also implies the end of a limited view based just *on the primacy of our own welfare or that of our immediate circle*. The sacrifice we have had to endure has been inflicted upon us by an apparently indifferent fate, but the *vibrant emptiness* that remains offers valuable space for a more creative attitude.

In each person there is set *an obscure faith*, which is fed by a hope that dwells in the soul – and this faith will surely become a real, living quality once we have given ourselves to the future life – *empty and battered* as we may be. This is *the act of saving faith that allows the Holy Spirit to enter our life and participate in our spiritual development.*

Those that have *the courage to persist* in their travail undergo a subtle inner transformation by which they are separated from material illusion and *grow slowly but inexorably into a life of joy, full of the grace of God.*

* * *

Much is expected of those to whom much is given. A ravaging illness which Martin underwent in later life would certainly seem to confirm the profound veracity of this age-old adage. Nothing, he wrote in one of his last full-length books, *changes one's life more radically than sudden dramatic adversity.* Black may seem more like white, while tragedy *may seem to open out a previously restricted personality into one of enormous potentiality.*

Around June 1997 – in his seventy-first year and with little warning – he suffered a catastrophic breakdown of health that led him by his own admission *to the solid portals of death.* It was a terrifying experience not only of almost total loss of physical capacity to render him forever more dependent on carers, but also one of prolonged loss of consciousness following increasing emotional distress, confusion and severe amnesia. It utterly transformed his outlook in such a way that he came to know beyond a shadow of doubt *that we are all immortal – not through our own deserts, but by the immeasurably great love of God.*

During this extended, near-death episode, requiring urgent hospital admission and a lengthy stay thereafter as he lay unconscious of his surroundings for weeks on end, he seemed to descend into *a vast pit of darkness* where he could 'sense' the souls of a vast concourse of people unknown to him. He seemed to be in hell, for the gloom was appalling and there seemed to be no hope anywhere; there was a total dissociation between his rational mind which was *shattered* and the deeper spiritual mind, which was *forlorn and lonely but entirely free*. Remarkably, however, there was a complete absence of fear – even though he felt desolate and bereft of all human contact.

He returned to normal consciousness one morning in mid-July with the sun shining gloriously through the window. It felt to him as if he had just woken up after a usual night's sleep. In fact he had lain unconscious for five weeks – and in the first few days of illness his life had hung in the balance.

After this severe attack, Martin was remarkably clear in mind, but he had completely lost the ability to walk and needed to begin to learn again. Even so, from that time on he would increasingly need a wheelchair and an altogether different way of life – still at home but now under constant care – beckoned. Ten years later – in October 2007 – Martin finally died from Parkinson's disease, with which the dramatic breakdown of his health was most certainly associated, but his final years were relatively happy and creative ones.

'My entire attitude to life has been changed by my "return from the portals of death". I am far less impatient with irritating people or disturbing circumstances than I was previously.' he wrote with characteristic conviction soon after these dramatic events.

'I have now acquired a degree of acceptance which makes every moment not only tolerable but even a joy in its own right. Another quite interesting change has been an acquisition of self-confidence, which was previously completely lacking in my character: I could not bear to hurt anybody's feelings and rejoiced in being well thought of by everybody. Indeed my apparent virtue had far too much self-interest attached to it. Now I am much more clear-spoken than I was previously, and the cripplingly low self-esteem of the past has been replaced by confidence and trust.'

Martin was doubtless sorely disappointed at the abrupt manner in which sudden illness had terminated his formal ministry as priest, but he was not a man to become embittered. All he wanted to do in the few years remaining to him was to be as helpful to others as he could, realising he was not special but *merely a frail fallible human being.* This knowledge was now for him *the real focus of happiness* and good enough reason for contentment despite his disability as he continued to fulfil his healing vocation while being well cared for in the peaceful sanctuary of his new home.

Chapter 26

The Dream

*People often wonder what the deceased do in the world beyond death.
The question is reasonable enough since our concept of intelligence
and independence shows itself in action that has an end in view. All
action starts in the mind, and in the afterlife, which is a mind world,
the action of the blessed departed is to pray for the souls of their less
fortunate brethren in the lower purgatorial realms and in hell – and
also for the distracted mortals on this side of the grave.*

*Prayer is a two-way communication: we help our living fellows
and those who are in a bad state after death, whereas the saints work
in the opposite direction. The earthbound souls are thus helped from
two directions...*

It is clear to me from some remarkably lucid dreams I have had
in my own life that Martin knew just what he was talking about
when he spoke without fear or favour about the subtle, astral
realms beyond the veil of death. He firmly believed that the traditional pictures of heaven *err too much in their static representation.*
Somehow the chosen have arrived and are in a state of peaceful
inanimation. He did not share this view – and furthermore it was
evidently not at all what he had in mind regarding the possibility
of his continuing ministry by the grace of God in the hereafter
when it was his turn to pass on.

Little more than two years before he suffered the catastrophic
breakdown in health, which brought his career as a priest in the
Church of England to an abrupt end, he had a vivid dream,
which further deepened his already considerable understanding
of the afterlife.

He seemed to have been involved in a road accident, and he
found himself clambering out of a rather shadowy car. The road

ahead was rough and he had to crawl forward to escape from some people in his way, but at last he reached the end of the road and found himself in a vast expanse of clear space. There were no road markings, but the space was taken up by diaphanous beings, whose shape resembled the human form, but without recognizable features. They seemed to cluster together in joyous groups, animated by a spirit of love that poured out into the atmosphere. They received Martin as one of their own – and he seemed to play along with them in their harmonious movement.

Then he began to wonder where he actually was. One of the company immediately seemed to sense his question and asked him in turn: 'Don't you know that you are dead?' Then it seemed he was being ushered to a great building for appraisal and instruction, but by this time he had become so excited that he was on the point of awakening in order to make immediately available this direct knowledge concerning the survival of personality after death.

Seldom had he woken up with such exhilaration and joy, and he could hardly wait to consider ideas for yet another book – about angels this time – until he realised he had barely enough definite material to fill even a single page of foolscap. That is how hard it is to write convincingly about things ethereal. Even so, before long, that book entitled, *Angels – Messengers of Grace,* did in 1995 eventually appear under his authorship, and comprehensive in scope – if somewhat daunting in readability – it certainly turned out to be.

Martin's enthralling dream and the book about angels that followed his vivid encounter with them demonstrated how the true self or soul of a person can receive clear intimations of a real life that *far exceeds the limitations of the rational mind without in any way failing to concede its place in dealing with the things of this world.* The true mystic, wrote Martin, is a very practical person, bringing the energies of God down to the world – but in this esoteric work one is not alone. Between the Godhead and creation there exists an order of beings that is spiritual in nature and also able to convey the divine energies to all that lives.

These mysterious beings are the angels – messengers bringing the light of God to men and forming part of a vast hierarchy. Martin would now apply himself in characteristically erudite and methodical fashion into researching this wondrous but somewhat archaic aspect of religion in all its minute detail as depicted throughout both the Old and New Testaments, while ensuring not to omit evidence of contemporary visitations either.

He, for his part, was convinced that the diaphanous ones whom he had seen were certainly angels. Who exactly it was he might have met in the great hall of learning to which he was being ushered was a matter of conjecture. Had he been *rather less impetuous,* he might conceivably have found out, but probably in his earthly state of spiritual understanding he was not yet eligible for a heavenly meeting. Perhaps, however, by the time he made the *great transition that we call death,* he would be better prepared for what was to come.

Whatever their origin, Martin was certain that angels form an essential link between human beings and God – and more universally between the whole created world and its creator. It would be an important day in his view when theologians decided to give the matter more attention, for then they would come closer to the divine source.

The fate of the world in no small measure depends on how responsibly humanity responds to the stark challenges it presently faces. If we stubbornly persist in attempting to proceed without reference to God – however he may be named – the more likely is our eventual self-destruction.

On the other hand, the sooner we are brave enough as a race to extend the range of our knowledge beyond the limits of the reasoning mind, and open up to the larger possibilities suggested by the reality of angels and all that pertains to them in the subtle, intermediate realms of existence, the more rapidly might we be able to move towards the conscious acknowledgement of the sacred dimension, from which all blessings flow.

* * *

Martin admitted to his readers that he had always found a peculiarly strong affinity with those who were soon to die, and he took pains to stress the importance of a quietly reverential attitude when spending time with the terminally ill. To be able to *pour out the love that is a presage of eternity* on someone who is about to make the great transition that we call death is one of the counsellor's greatest joys, he wrote.

He had discovered too that quite often his ministering work did not end with his last visit to his friends and parishioners at great time of need in home or hospital. On occasion he had become aware during his sleep of actually accompanying them to the threshold of the afterlife – popularly symbolized as a door. They were admitted, but he repeatedly was turned back.

He had always rather envied these departing souls, for he had come to know that existence 'on the other side' was much easier than it is here, where we face endless difficulties so necessary for soul growth – but ones that may not exist in other realms.

In essence our life on earth is a preparation for the life beyond death when we will finally be able to directly approach the understanding of eternity. But eternity, Martin emphasised, is not simply a future experience in store for us. It is in fact *our constant dwelling place even at this moment in time* and we would know this if only we were more fully aware of the glory that constantly surrounds us.

The doors of our inner perception are often so firmly shut that we are impervious to all impressions except the coarsely material kind – no bad thing since *our place of growth is where we find ourselves and the tools of operation are the circumstances at hand.*

But if only we were aware – albeit dimly – of the destination ahead of us while we were *about our earthly business,* we could act altogether *more effectively and joyously.* We would probably be less grasping and more compassionate, less demanding and more solicitous about the wants and needs of other people. In this manner the *apparently great divide* between our earthly existence and the faintly perceived life beyond death might be narrowed and therefore more easily bridged.

There is, significantly, Martin acknowledged, *no incontrovertible evidence of survival of death,* but somehow *we begin to know the secret of survival as we come to a deeper knowledge of our own depths.*

When we begin to see every action and relationship of ours, every possession and experience as *both the way towards eternal life and a sacrament of that life in the present moment,* we are beginning to glimpse what true abundance means. The spiritual counsellor – the one whose role it is to focus and channel wisdom on behalf of his client – needs to know thoroughly this fullness of life in order to transmit that knowledge to those seeking his help. This he does *not so much by exhortation as by his transparency, not so much by description as by his radiance.*

In the end, Martin concluded, an authentic spiritual guide does not presume to describe what has been seen *at the peak of the mountain of illumination* – instead such a vision needs to be enshrined in his or her personality and brought down to earth. The true joy of counselling is to be able to guide a person on the road that leads to completion – and this guidance *is an aspect of companionship, not leadership.*

This is the kind of invaluable support that Martin Israel offered all those who trusted his advice and were prepared to put it into practice with patience and goodwill.

Chapter 27

Truth and Illusion

In the end the state of heaven has to include everyone because the absence of even one creature diminishes it, and it is therefore not completely heavenly. No one in heaven can be in a state of joyous abandon with the knowledge that there are creatures in distress anywhere in the universe. The openness of the soul in heaven brings with it a sensitivity to all the world's pain, and with that awareness comes an ineradicable desire to relieve it.

It is indeed true that the souls of the virtuous are at peace with God, but their work is to bring the knowledge of that spiritual peace down to the turmoil of the outside world. To leave heavenly peace is a great sacrifice, but its motive is pure love: to bring that peace to whomsover will receive it at the present moment in time. There is no greater work than this, for it prepares the work for Christ's second coming.

How thoroughly impracticable is this representation of heaven in the eyes of worldly experience, but it continues to form the basis of all genuinely moral behaviour. And in the dark shadow cast by the immense refugee crisis that has engulfed Europe in the wake of savage and intractable warfare in the Middle East and far beyond, his words certainly appear incredibly apposite too – while the essential principles of mercy that uphold them have never been more urgently required. It is salutary for us now to consider that this was Martin Israel's firm stance – an expression of his most profound convictions. So indeed must it remain his enduring message for our deeply troubled time, however unlikely it is that love and non-violence alone can ever resolve what has now become a seemingly endless crisis of global proportions.

* * *

In whatever he wrote following his acute illness and terrifying near-death experience, in which he experienced the chaotic *darkness of hell*, Martin struck a very different tone from earlier in his ministry. Although always compassionate, previously, he sometimes came across as stern, even combative, but in the last decade of his life he seemed altogether more mellow, kind and lenient – well aware of human nature in all its frailty, but less inclined to sit in final judgement.

Perhaps the emphatic quotation, with which I have chosen to begin this penultimate chapter and which seems so relevant to modern day concerns, may be regarded as his last testament, since it stands alone as an expression of universality and tolerance – even though it is presented in very particular Christian terminology, and accordingly may be difficult for some people to accept at face value.

For me nevertheless, as an errant pilgrim brought up in the Christian tradition – estranged from Christianity until becoming reconciled once again to the authentic faith of my birth – these are words marked out by compassionate, moderation and plain common sense. Of this I am in no doubt and perhaps interested readers, whatever their persuasion, will come to the same conclusion if they do not just take my word for it, but continue to explore the astonishing range of Martin's written work after finishing this introductory study of his unassuming life and incisive teachings.

Dedicated Christian priest, assiduous in his duties as he undoubtedly was, he always retained a clear awareness of the relative nature of both religious creed, as well as secular and scientific belief systems, insisting on the absolute need for discernment as he skirted the pitfalls of illusion to discover the abiding truth in the midst of constant change.

'It is obvious to me,' he wrote 'that the really important things of life cannot be proven in any way other than experience. When people try to bring religion and science together they nearly always distort the scientific view to suit themselves. The tangible cannot easily be connected to the intangible, yet it is by truth that has come to one on a very personal level that one in the end leads one's life.'

With the wry humour so characteristic of him, he then queried: What for instance could be said for sure about a person like himself? On a personal level remarkably little, although he was by that point in time an elderly man with considerable experience.

'Even my appearance as I see in photographs does not entirely match up to the face that confronts me day by day as I shave it,' he acknowledged. More often than not he was of serious demeanour, yet I can well imagine him now, beaming with quiet merriment as he made such an off the cuff remark.

By this simple example one could see that although truth does not change, the subject of it is undergoing constant remodelling, but what concerned him particularly was the inner attitude one adopted and how crucial that was regarding the quest for lasting happiness.

'In the end it matters little what you think about me externally, whether I am handsome or ugly for instance, but what you feel about my character and therefore my integrity is quite a different matter.'

It seemed to Martin that truth on a moral level is *universal in scope* – the various great world religions *set their finest practices in daily living and do not merely preach it on suitable occasions.* It was all too easy to cloak one's deficiencies under a torrent of words full of sincerity, but lacking in real substance – for it is by the fruit of one's actions that one is really known.

Ultimately though we also need to consider the mysterious part fate plays in determining how we live out our life. Martin was in no doubt that destiny formed his life before he was born.

In his case he knew even as a small boy that he would never marry – and incredibly his whole outlook as a child and adolescent was that of a mature adult. In a peculiar way, he admitted, he had never really been young at all.

He felt he had not chosen Christianity, because his spirituality was *essentially universalistic,* but somehow it was decreed that he should embrace the Christian faith – and he had followed in complete obedience, despite the fact that neither Christian history nor the Christians he knew personally were especially inspiring.

'I did what was required of me and I do not regret my obedience either,' he wrote.

The teachings of Jesus were for him undoubtedly *beyond compare* – the only problem was their *impracticability for common humanity.* If only everyone could follow the precepts of the Sermon on the Mount, the world would be as the heaven described in orthodox religion, but how many millennia would have to pass before that wonderful state comes to pass?

Now at the end of his career, Martin could see plainly why he *as a mere nobody* had been called upon to practise preaching, writing, the deliverance work of exorcism and counselling as a Christian minister. He had been *given a perfect platform for enunciating eternal truths and to a very limited extent even living them.* This ought to apply to every minister, whether Christian or belonging to some other great faith.

'It is on people like me and them that the ultimate survival of humanity depends,' he noted, but the temptations towards self-agrandizement and power could be insurmountable without genuine humility and even an innate sense of low esteem as had been his lot.

So, therefore, his Christian ministry had certainly not been an attempt to escape from Jewish stigmatization and he had never attempted to change his ultra-Jewish surname into something more generally acceptable as his parents had suggested before he came to England from South Africa. He definitely did not see himself as a convert to Christianity, for he was no missionary and the very idea of enforced conversion he found utterly distasteful.

He had rather simply *fulfilled a destiny which was prearranged*, regarding himself as neither better nor worse than other people.

Martin believed that God has given to each one of us, as it were, *the tools pertinent to our particular personality*, but how we employ them is entirely up to us. Therefore, he concluded, destiny has a *strongly foreordained aspect*, but how it unfolds depends upon our individual response to the challenges we face.

Chapter 28

Intimations of Joy

The counsellor is the instrument of the Holy Spirit. His work is to impart the wisdom of God in words of gentle understanding to the perplexed, the harassed and the fearful. Those who are perplexed see the light of God's purpose in their lives, the harassed are given the balm of God's peace, and the fearful are filled with the radiance of God's love.

As you approach the end of this study of the life and teachings of Martin Israel – short on biographical detail perhaps but hopefully abundant in respect of valuable insights – you will find in the quotation from his writings given here an immaculate summary of the sacred task with which this unassuming doctor and priest had been entrusted as a minister of healing.

But there is an essential quality missing from his description, to which he had already referred while reflecting on the profound vocation of spiritual counselling, but which I have not yet included. That is the vital element of joy, which *is the soul's unending song as it goes about God's business in unselfconscious delight.*

A natural sense of communion with the creation in union with the Creator is *the essence of joy*, wrote Martin, and the business of God *is the healing and transmutation of all that is distorted and awry*, so it may be made afresh in the divine image in which it was originally fashioned. Unity with God is finally recognised by the spiritual seeker as no longer a theological affirmation, but a fact of existence proved by the transformation of the personality.

It is seen in a wondrous alteration of outlook, not accomplished solely by human intervention but ultimately by the mysterious power of the Holy Spirit. Such a turning about of consciousness on its axis marks the crossing of a significant threshold at the beginning of an invigorated life of faith.

It was the great privilege of all those involved in the counselling process, further explained Martin, to lead the person seeking guidance *to the joy of recognition that all is well for those who put their trust in the creative potentiality of life.* The counsellor's soul should radiate that joy – he should so far beyond the limitations of his own understanding in fact that *his vision can glimpse the glory beyond rational definition.*

Then the one guiding can communicate directly with the soul of the other person, who comes for help. In this manner *joy kindles the fearful personality with trust that issues forth in fruitful endeavour, so that its soul blazes triumphantly in a new work enlightened by the spirit within.*

And the amazing thing is that this joy prevails even when *circumstances are threatening and failure seems certain to crown all our efforts.* Even if this world were to *go up in smoke* joy would not end – Martin assures us of that.

The reason for this is that joy is *of a different order of excellence* from pleasure or even happiness, both of which depend on material well-being and are related to circumstances. It is obviously hard to be happy when one is ill, in financial distress, or surrounded by social turmoil or political upheaval. The intention of counselling is to set before each person the basic truth of his own being – that God lies within him and consequently he is no longer fully dependent on outer help. Authentic guidance such as Martin offered, does not so much dispose of problems but transfigure them in the light of good counsel and love to *a radiance of universal health...*

As health emerges unobtrusively from the depths of the purged personality, so does joy hesitantly radiate from the open soul, now cleared of egotistical barriers and cleansed of the effect of adverse conditioning. The emergence of joy is like the slow advent of the

*rising sun on a distant horizon: it starts as a delicate, suffused glow
that seems gradually to gain the courage of momentum until its
light fully heralds the dawn of a new day. This joy is a confirmation
of a faith made real by God's mighty healing act and fully established
in a life of health.*

This is the end-point of Martin Israel's teachings. Joy cannot be
cultivated as such, but is *evoked* as we attain the freedom
necessary to establish our true spiritual identity. In Christian
terms it simply means this: every single person without exception
is a child of God made in the image of Jesus Christ. The more we
grow in stature into the fully actualised person we are intended
to be, the more all our disabilities fall into place in the scheme of
our life's unfolding – and as this happens, each of our failings
contributes mysteriously in its healed aspect to our full life in
God.

*When we are nothing, we are everything, for then we know Him as
the supreme No-Thing from Whom all that exists finds its creative
source. He is known to us as love, which is exquisitely personal in
its concern, and we respond with the soul's song of joy. The end is
peace – to do God's will in harmony with each other in His presence.
The soul that has found its rest in God... is at peace with God, with
its fellows and with itself. It does as it wills since it is moved by love.*

CHRISTIAN
ALTERNATIVE

Throughout the two thousand years of Christian tradition there
have been, and still are, groups and individuals that exist in the
margins and upon the edge of faith. But in Christianity's
contrapuntal history it has often been these outcasts and
pioneers that have forged contemporary orthodoxy out of
former radicalism as belief evolves to engage with and
encompass the ever-changing social and scientific realities. Real
faith lies not in the comfortable certainties of the Orthodox, but
somewhere in a half-glimpsed hinterland on the dirt track to
Emmaus, where the Death of God meets the Resurrection, where
the supernatural Christ meets the historical Jesus, and where the
revolution liberates both the oppressed and the oppressors.

Welcome to Christian Alternative... a space at the edge where
the light shines through.